Backroad Bicycling in the Finger Lakes Region

Backroad Bicycling in the Finger Lakes Region

Fourth Edition

MARK ROTH AND
SALLY WALTERS

Updated by the
TNMC Bike Club

30 Tours for Road and
Mountain Bikes

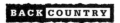

Backcountry Guides
Woodstock, Vermont

AN INVITATION TO THE READER Although it is unlikely that the roads you cycle on these tours will change much with time, some road signs, landmarks, and other items may. If you find that such changes have occurred on these routes, please let the author and publisher know, so that corrections may be made in future editions. Other comments and suggestions are also welcome. Address all correspondence to: Editor, Backroad Bicycling Series, Backcountry Guides, P.O. Box 748, Woodstock, VT 05091.

Fourth Edition
Previously published as *30 Bicycle Tours in the Finger Lakes Region*

ISBN 0-88150-605-2
ISSN 1547-3260

Cover and interior design by Bodenweber Design
Composition by Final Proof Design & Publishing
Cover photograph by the TNMC
Maps by Jeff Goodwin, © 2004 The Countryman Press

Published by Backcountry Guides, a division of The Countryman Press, P.O. Box 748, Woodstock, Vermont 05091

Distributed by W.W. Norton & Company, Inc., 500 Fifth Avenue, New York, NY 10110

Printed in the United States of America

To the memory of Rose Roth, Sam Roth, Anne Walters, and Oliver P. Walters

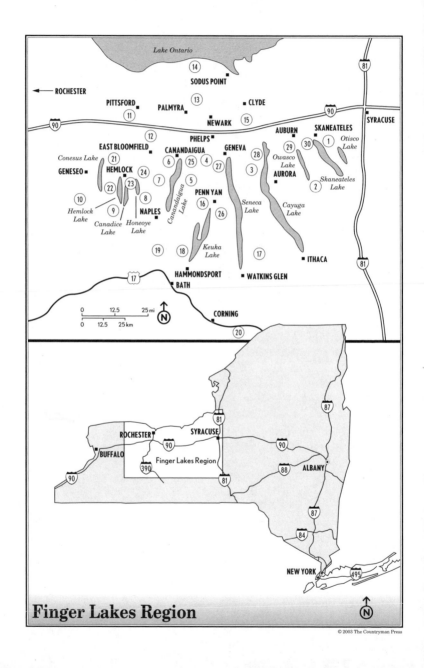

Finger Lakes Region

© 2003 The Countryman Press

CONTENTS

ACKNOWLEDGMENTS For their assistance in making our travels more enjoyable or our research more complete, we would like to thank Clare Bavis, Noreen Black, Bruce Gilman, Richard Hubbard, Henry Maus, Robert Moody, Winnie Peer, Marjory Allen Perez, Marvin Rapp, Betsy and David Schlesinger, Teresa Thurn, William and Robert Vierhile, Pat Vitalone, and Marian and John Winkelman. We are also grateful for the help given by the directors and staffs of area historical societies and museums, particularly those of the Cayuga Museum of History and Art; the Geneva Historical Society; the Livingston County Historical Society; the Ontario County Historical Society; and the Yates County Historical Society. Most of all, our appreciation goes to editors Susan Edwards and Justine Rathbun for their thoroughness and fine sense of style.

—Mark Roth and Sally Walters

TNMC The TNMC (Thursday Night Men's Club) was founded in 1989 in Bristol, New York. Members of the club meet weekly to share our enjoyment of biking and skiing in the Finger Lakes region.

Updating this book was a wonderful project that involved our entire club. We hope you will enjoy the various rides in this book as much as we have. The club would like to thank the authors, Mark Roth and Sally Walters, for allowing us the opportunity to update their book. The club also thanks the folks at The Countryman Press for their guidance and support and for making this book available again to those who enjoy cycling the Finger Lakes region. Good pedaling!

BACKROAD BICYCLE TOURS AT A GLANCE

RIDE	STARTING POINT	DISTANCE (MILES)
1. Skaneateles	Sherwood Inn	25 miles
2. Owasco Lake	Auburn	38 miles
3. Finger Lakes Heartland	Geneva	115 miles
4. Geneva–Phelps–Gorham	Geneva	37 miles
5. Canandaigua–Vine Valley	Canandaigua	26 miles
6. Canandaigua—City and Lake	Canandaigua	18 miles
7. The Bristol Hills	Cheshire	24 miles
8. Naples–Honeoye Lake	Naples	30 miles
9. Canadice and Hemlock Lakes	Hemlock	29 miles
10. Genesee Valley and Gorge	Geneseo	57 miles

TERRAIN	DIFFICULTY	HIGHLIGHTS
Rolling hills	Moderate to easy	Otisco Lake, Roosevelt Hall, polo grounds
Level riding with gradual hills	Easy to moderate	Fillmore Glen State Park; Emerson Park; historic homes
Mostly rolling	Easy to strenuous	Wells, Ithaca, Hobart, and William Smith Colleges; winery; Women's Rights National Historical Park
Level with gently rolling hills	Easy	Rural farm landscapes; beautiful, historic Geneva
Level to rolling	Moderate	Views of lake and vineyards; Vine Valley
Flat; some low hills	Easy to moderate	Sonnenberg Gardens and Mansion; elegant old homes; country scenery
Rolling to hilly	Moderate to strenuous	Rugged, attractive scenery; antiques dealers; Bristol Mountain
Low rolling hills	Moderate	Nature reserves; art galleries; winery
Rolling to hilly	Moderate to strenuous	Country riding in sparsely settled countryside; winery
Varied	Easy to strenuous	Genesee River Gorge; museums

RIDE	STARTING POINT	DISTANCE
11. Pittsford–Erie Canal	Bushnells Basin	19 miles
12. East Bloomfield–Powder Mills Park	East Bloomfield	32 miles
13. Mormon Country	Hill Cumorah	29 miles
14. Lake Ontario Shores	Sodus Point	40 miles
15. Montezuma Marsh	Montezuma National Wildlife Refuge	39 miles
16. Bluff Point	Penn Yan	27 or 19 miles
17. Watkins Glen–Hector Wineries	Watkins Glen State Park	21 miles
18. Hammondsport Wineries	Hammondsport	3–17 miles
19. Steuben County Valleys	Bath	28 or 38 miles
20. Corning–Harris Hill	Corning	32 miles

TERRAIN	DIFFICULTY	HIGHLIGHTS
Flat towpath; low, hilly terrain	Easy to moderate	Erie Canal towpath; quaint village center; parks
Small hills	Moderate	Rural woodland riding; Powder Mills Park; trout hatchery
Low, rolling hills	Moderate	Hill Cumorah; Martin Harris's farm; canal park
Mostly level; some low hills	Easy	Fruit orchards; cobblestone houses
Low hills; some level stretches	Easy to moderate	Bird-watching; canal parks
Level to slightly undulating	Mostly easy; some moderate	Quiet lakeside riding; Bluff Point; Keuka Lake State Park; winery
Gradual ascents	Easy to moderate and descents	Watkins Glen State Park and International Race Track; wineries; Finger Lakes National Forest
Mostly level	Easy	Wineries
Gentle climbs; some level terrain	Moderate	Cycling through rural, sparsely settled countryside
Flat; one big hill	Easy	Sailplane rides; National Soaring Museum; Museum of Glass

RIDE	STARTING POINT	DISTANCE
21. Conesus Lake Loop	Conesus Motel	19 miles
22. Hemlock Lake Loop	Intersection of NY 15A and US 20A	27 miles
23. Canadice Lake Loop	Intersection of Canadice Lake and Burch Hill Roads	13 miles
24. Honeoye Lake Loop	Honeoye Central School	18 miles
25. Canandaigua Lake Loop	Canandaigua	44 miles
26. Keuka Lake Loop	Penn Yan Academy	45 miles
27. Seneca Lake Loop	Lakeshore Park, Geneva	77 miles
28. Cayuga Lake Loop	Cayuga Lake State Park	90 miles
29. Owasco Lake Loop	Emerson Park	32 miles
30. Skaneateles Lake Loop	Skaneateles	40 miles

TERRAIN	DIFFICULTY	HIGHLIGHTS
Easy	Easy	Lake views
Moderate to difficult	Moderate to difficult	Winery, rural cycling
Moderate; one long climb	Moderate	Rural woodlands
Gently rolling	Easy	Swimming
Moderate	Moderate	Wineries, arts & crafts
Moderate hills, then mostly level	Moderate to easy	Wineries, Glenn Curtiss museum
Moderate	Moderate	Watkins Glen, wineries
Rolling	Easy to moderate	Cornell, Ithaca College, Wells College
Easy to moderate	Easy to moderate	Fillmore Glen State Park
Moderately difficult	Moderately difficult	Historic Skaneateles, arts & crafts

INTRODUCTION What's special about New York State's Finger Lakes region? The narrow, finger-shaped lakes themselves are surely the primary attraction. There are similar groups of lakes in the world—in the Yukon, Chile, Sweden, and New Zealand—but none closer than an expensive plane ride away. Other outstanding natural features include the highest waterfalls east of the Rockies, cascades, glens, and the Genesee River Gorge. The area is small and topography changes quickly, so cycling is never monotonous.

The Finger Lakes is the oldest commercial winemaking area in the United States, today second only to California in production; about three dozen wineries welcome visitors for tours or tastings. Vineyards scale seemingly impossible slopes, highlighting pleasingly varied pastoral scenes—from fields of small buckwheat plants to acres of golden sunflowers. Lakes and hills, farms and colleges, forests and fields, cities and hamlets—all can be visited in a day of leisurely cycling, with time out for a swim.

Two of the Finger Lakes are very long, but the other nine are from 3 to 16 miles; a car can pass them by in minutes, yet they can be your companions for days of cycling. On a bike you can smell the spring sweetness of fruit blossoms and the fall ripeness of grapes, hear the goldfinches, or feel the temperature drop as you approach one of the deep, cool lakes on a summer day. Enhancing the delight of cycling here is an extensive network of paved, well-maintained back roads with very light traffic. (When asked about the seemingly endless miles of roads serving only scattered farms, a young farmer smiled. "You'd be surprised," he said, "how many farmers are town road supervisors.")

Most cyclists' moods change: Sometimes we pedal quickly, exhilarated with pure motion; sometimes we stop and putter— swim, explore a path or museum, or pick wild berries. You can use the maps and route directions to ride fast on uncrowded, scenic roads; or you can take your time, reading our background paragraphs to learn a bit about the history, geology, architecture, and personalities of the Finger Lakes. This book is intended for all moods.

THE TERRAIN   The 11 bodies of water that give the Finger Lakes region its name and special character range from 3-mile-long Canadice to 40-mile Cayuga. In general, the northern part of the area is rather level, with many places of cultural or historical interest in and around such small cities as Auburn, Seneca Falls, Geneva, and Canandaigua. The southern ends of the lakes are tucked among high hills; towns are fewer and smaller, the scenery is more spectacular, and cycling is more strenuous.

The land between the lakes is characterized by forested rolling hills and farmed valleys. The field mosaic includes pasture for dairy herds, vineyards, orchards, and hay, wheat, oats, rye, beans, tomatoes, and other vegetables. Maximum relief is seldom over 1,000 feet—the highest point is Gannett Hill (2,256 feet), west of Canandaigua Lake. Since the hills and lakes trend north–south, riding in these directions is usually easier than riding east–west.

Greatly simplified, and skipping an odd few million years here and there, the Finger Lakes came about something like this: Thousands of feet of sedimentary rock (mostly limestone, sandstone, and shale) formed under a shallow inland sea. The land rose, sank, rose again, and was worn down and dissected by streams. Then, during the Ice Age, two separate glacial advances deepened and widened the already existing north–south stream valleys, forming the beds of the present lakes. Some of the gouging was extraordinarily powerful—the bottom of Seneca Lake, for example, is almost 200 feet below sea level. East–west streams were not deepened so much; left high above the new valley floors, but not dry, they form the many waterfalls and glens for which

the area is known. The final gift of the glaciers was the Valley Heads Moraine, hills of glacial debris, damming the lakes to the south.

Of the Finger Lakes climate, an 18th-century traveler wrote: "No part of America is better suited for dairy farms; for at no time is the weather so hot but butter can be made and preserved." May through September is the prime cycling season, though April always has some perfect days, and comfortable weather continues through October, with fall colors peaking about the middle of that month. Rain is distributed evenly through the warmer months, and high temperatures seldom exceed 90 degrees Fahrenheit. Cities can absorb considerable heat, but in the countryside cool nights are the rule.

THE TOURS The tours described here range from a few level miles to a 115-mile ride, though most are between 25 and 40 miles. All end where they begin. Some rides are along lakeshores, offering chances to swim or fish; others climb high ridges between the lakes, with panoramic views. You can ride through orchards and pick apples, or by vineyards and visit wineries. You can choose rural rides where the only evidence you'll see of man is as farmer or logger, or tours that can include visits to historic buildings, museums, antiques shops, crafts fairs, colleges, and universities.

In selecting a tour, the first criterion is probably length. Next, you might consider the characterization of the cycling: easy, moderate, strenuous. This judgment is based primarily on the height and steepness of hills to be climbed, but it isn't only hills that make cycling difficult. The road surface quality counts for a lot, and the direction and strength of the wind is even more important. The introductory paragraphs before each tour give a quick preview of what that tour offers. If a tour seems appealing, read on.

It is best to read to the end of a tour before you begin, to know whether to bring food, a bathing suit, or other special equipment. At intersections, continue straight unless a turn is indicated. Sometimes a direction to continue straight is given, and sometimes not, depending on the likelihood of confusion and the distance from the last turn. To avoid compounding errors and to eliminate the need for a cyclometer, calculate your mileage from one point to the next, rather than from the start of the tour. Signposting can change (signs are swept away by snowplowing each winter), but you should find roads where we describe them. Since more roads are paved each year, you may occasionally find a paved road where our directions indicate a gravel one. Road names and numbers at unsignposted corners are given so that when you come upon a sign farther along, you can confirm your position.

Lunch or midtour rest stops are often suggested, and occasionally restaurants near a tour's finish are mentioned. Overnight accommodations are detailed for the multiday tours; elsewhere lodgings are suggested when they are of particular interest. Cyclists may be especially interested in bed-and-breakfast places that have sprung up in recent years. Brochures and guides listing many of the bed-and-breakfasts and small inns can be obtained from the Finger Lakes Association, 309 Lake Street, Penn Yan 14527 (315-536-7488 or 1-800-548-4386). For more information visit www.fingerlakes.org or www.visitfingerlakes.com, or call Finger Lakes Tourism at 1-800-548-4386.

MAPS Good maps of the Finger Lakes region are produced by Map Works, Inc., of Rochester, New York. They offer maps in a variety of formats, including a small laminated version (but this does not have the detail of smaller roads). These maps can be found in bookstores, convenience stores, grocery stores, and drugstores throughout the Finger Lakes region; or you can order them by calling Map Works at 1-800-822-6277 or by visiting their Web site, www.mapworksinc.com.

In addition, ordinary oil company maps of New York State can be used to find the starting points of these tours. Other good maps to supplement the ones in this book are produced by each county's highway department. These can be obtained by writing to the addresses given at the end of this book. The U.S. Geological Survey produces excellent maps, but the scales covering the Finger Lakes fall between the chairs: The 1:24,000 or 7.5' series (1" equals 2,000') has great detail but requires almost one hundred sheets to cover the area; while the 1:250,000 series covers the region in only two sheets but does not show most of the small roads used on these tours. These two sheets of the latter series (the Elmira and Rochester quadrangles) are invaluable, however, for getting an overall picture of the terrain. Maps can be ordered from the U.S. Geological Survey, Map Distribution Branch, Box 25286, Denver Federal Center, Denver, CO 80225.

BICYCLING SAFETY AND EQUIPMENT Whenever possible, tours follow quiet country roads or highways with shoulders. Still, following a described tour or being on a bike route is no guarantee of safety. Alertness and good judgment are always needed—even on little-used farm roads. Backcountry residents can get accustomed to driving rather fast on their own roads; from experience they expect little traffic, and may be ill prepared to encounter cyclists.

Common sense should govern riding behavior. Keeping to the right with the traffic, signaling turns, and obeying other traffic regulations are required by law. And remember the old joke about the 500-pound pet gorilla who gets to sit anywhere he pleases; a 3,000-pound motor vehicle is not going to be pushed around by a

30-pound bicycle. So ride accordingly.

For short and easy tours, any bike will do. Covering longer distances or hilly terrain is less difficult on a lightweight bike with a choice of gears; newer bikes have anywhere from 12 to 21 gears. Better-made, lighter bikes increase efficiency and speed; they tackle hills more easily, and they generally have better brakes for safer descents. If you're unsure of your brakes, or any other bike part, and are not inclined to tinker, have your bike checked by a competent mechanic.

Cyclists who venture beyond convenient walking distance from assistance ought at least to be able to repair a flat tire. And carry a pump! Clear instructions for basic repairs can be found in the books on bicycling listed under Additional Reading at the end of this book. Bike parts or assistance may be found at the bike shops listed at the end of each tour. It's wise to call first, to be sure the shop is open and has the parts or skills you need.

20 TOURS

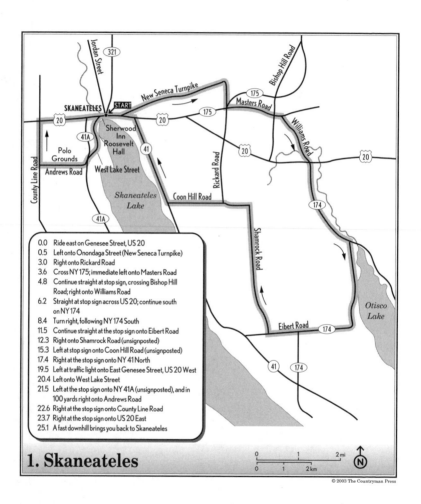

0.0	Ride east on Genesee Street, US 20
0.5	Left onto Onondaga Street (New Seneca Turnpike)
3.0	Right onto Rickard Road
3.6	Cross NY 175; immediate left onto Masters Road
4.8	Continue straight at stop sign, crossing Bishop Hill Road; right onto Williams Road
6.2	Straight at stop sign across US 20; continue south on NY 174
8.4	Turn right, following NY 174 South
11.5	Continue straight at the stop sign onto Eibert Road
12.3	Right onto Shamrock Road (unsignposted)
15.3	Left at stop sign onto Coon Hill Road (unsignposted)
17.4	Right at the stop sign onto NY 41 North
19.5	Left at traffic light onto East Genesee Street, US 20 West
20.4	Left onto West Lake Street
21.5	Left at the stop sign onto NY 41A (unsignposted), and in 100 yards right onto Andrews Road
22.6	Right at the stop sign onto County Line Road
23.7	Right at the stop sign onto US 20 East
25.1	A fast downhill brings you back to Skaneateles

1. Skaneateles

Skaneateles

- **DISTANCE**: 25 miles; moderate to easy cycling
- **TERRAIN**: Rolling hills with gradual inclines
- **COUNTY MAP**: Onondaga

The village of Skaneateles, the "Eastern Gateway to the Finger Lakes," makes as pleasant an introduction to the region as one could wish. Its quaint main street curves around the north end of the lake that William Seward, Lincoln's secretary of state, called "the most beautiful body of water in the world." The village has excellent eating places, a historic inn, a lakefront enhanced by two landscaped parks, and the most impressive array of 19th-century houses and estates in the region.

The cycling route makes a figure-eight pattern: a morning loop through farmland to the east, a lunch break in Skaneateles, then a short loop through the country of the horsey set, passing the polo grounds where matches are played on Sunday afternoons in summer. You'll ride beside the two easternmost Finger Lakes, Otisco and Skaneateles, and get panoramic views from the high ridge between them. Fishing is possible in either lake, while swimming is most convenient in Skaneateles.

The tour starts in front of the Sherwood Inn in Skaneateles.

0.0 From the Sherwood Inn, ride east (with the lake to your right) on Genesee Street, US 20.

The present Sherwood Inn traces its origin to an 1807 building used to feed and lodge passengers traveling on Isaac Sherwood's stagecoach line. It was a colorful *era of fast horses and faster profits; in one year Sherwood took in more than $60,000 just for carrying the mail.*

It is easy to wax romantic imagining the old days of sleek four-horse teams, daring drivers and blaring horns, country inns with brass and candles and venison steak. Thurlow Weed, who traveled the Genesee Road in 1824, adds details often overlooked: "In country inns, a traveler who objected to a stranger as a bedfellow was regarded as unreasonably fastidious. Nothing was more common, after a passenger had retired, than to be awakened by the landlord, who appeared with a tallow candle, showing a stranger into your bed."

Skaneateles has many restaurants, from world famous and expensive to luncheonettes. Groceries are easily obtained but are perhaps superfluous, as the 20-mile morning loop can bring you back to town before lunchtime.

0.5 Turn left onto Onondaga Street, which is called New Seneca Turnpike outside the village.

In 1800 the state legislature chartered the Seneca Road and Turnpike Company to build and maintain a road from the home of John House in Utica to the courthouse in Canandaigua, over the route of the old Genesee Road. Tollgates, some with pikes to turn, were every 10 miles; a two-horse wagon paid 12½ cents. Any wagon with wheels more than 12 inches wide traveled free; it functioned as a roller-compactor for the roadway, while narrow, faster wheels cut ruts. Isaac Sherwood placed his inn near the junction of the two main east–west roads across the state, the Seneca and Cherry Valley Turnpikes.

3.0 Turn right onto Rickard Road.

3.6 At the stop sign, cross NY 175; then immediately turn left onto Masters Road.

4.8 Continue straight at the stop sign, crossing Bishop Hill Road; in 50 yards turn right onto Williams Road.

6.2 Go straight at the stop sign across US 20, to continue south on NY 174.

8.4 Turn right, following NY 174 South and signs to Skaneateles and Borodino.

For a closer look at Otisco Lake, you can delay turning right here and ride farther on the road to the left, which gives access to Otisco's east side. The area just past the dam is popular with anglers.

Polo is played each Sunday afternoon at 3 in Skaneateles.

11.5 After staying on NY 174 as it climbs and turns west, away from Otisco, continue straight at the stop sign onto Eibert Road.

Growing wild in abandoned fields and hedgerows hereabouts you may see a tall, thistlelike plant with a 2- to 3-inch spiky head called teasel. Now considered a weed, from 1835 until early in the 20th century teasel was a lucrative crop for area farmers. The teasel was used to raise the nap on wool cloth. Today manufacturers use wire brushes, even though they are said to do an inferior job. Skaneateles was once the world center of teasel production, with six factories and more than 500 acres supplying the market. While cultivation continues in Europe, the last commercial crop was harvested here in 1956.

12.3 Turn right onto Shamrock Road (unsignposted).

15.3 Turn left at the stop sign onto Coon Hill Road (unsignposted—Shamrock ends at Coon Hill Road).

17.4 After a long downhill, turn right at the stop sign onto NY 41 North.

19.5 Turn left at the traffic light onto East Genesee Street, US 20 West. *On the left, the Stella Maris retreat house was once owned by the Smiths, who founded the Smith-Corona typewriter company.*

20.4 After passing Skaneateles's center, turn left onto West Lake Street. *Lunch in Skaneateles can range from groceries alfresco in a lakeside park to a gourmet meal at the Sherwood Inn, where the fare would astound old Isaac's patrons, accustomed to "salt meat" for dinner and "for supper still more salt meat and coffee." Monday through Saturday the Sherwood serves lunch 11:30 AM–4 PM; call ahead to check Sunday's dining times. Casually dressed cyclists can enjoy the regular luncheon menu in the tavern.*

With its back to the Skaneateles Lake outlet, the Old Stone Mill restaurant occupies the handsome limestone building in which the Talcot Milling Company ground flour from 1842 to 1969. The outlet was once lined with factories and mills; almost a dozen distilleries converted local grains to more easily transported whiskey. These businesses were served, as were tourists, by what was perhaps the shortest railroad in America, a 5-mile line that ended in front of the Talcot Mill.

The houses along West Lake Street, representing a variety of architectural styles, form perhaps the best lineup of large old houses in the Finger Lakes. The centerpiece is the white Greek Revival mansion known as Roosevelt Hall. Built in 1839, and once owned by Samuel Montgomery Roosevelt, a cousin of Theodores, the house now belongs to the Christian Brothers Order.

21.5 Past the country club, turn left at the stop sign onto NY 41A (unsignposted), and in 100 yards turn right onto Andrews Road, following a sign to the polo grounds.
In a couple of hundred yards you'll see the bright green of the polo grounds to your right. Matches are played every Sunday afternoon in July and August at 3 PM; admission is $2 per car, with no charge for bikes. Once considered good exercise and training for battle, this ancient and exotic game is played on a field 300 yards long, covering the area of nine football fields. The informal setting lets you get so close you can hear the horses snort and the crack of mallets striking the wooden ball. An announcer gives a useful introduction to the sport and play-by-play commentary.

22.6 Turn right at the stop sign onto County Line Road.

23.7 Turn right at the stop sign onto US 20 East. On the right you will pass Mirbeau (315-685-5006), a full-service spa hotel with French château-style architecture in a provincial country-estate setting.

25.1 A fast downhill will soon bring you back to the village of Skaneateles. *You can swim in the purest lake water in the state (Syracuse residents drink it) at Clift Park, directly across from the Sherwood Inn; a $2 fee is charged.*

The inn has 16 guest rooms, decorated in various 19th-century styles, with rates from $85 to $170, including Continental breakfast. Excellent dinners, chosen from a largely Continental menu and a long wine list, are served in four dining rooms, all carefully furnished in Colonial style.

Many people who won't even try to pronounce Skaneateles (on local tongues it sounds like Skinny-atlas) known for its famous restaurant, The Krebs. It's been here since 1899 and has had many famous guests. Family-style dinners are served daily from 6 PM, and a brunch is served on Sunday.

Skaneateles may remind sailing enthusiasts of the Lightning Class boat, which was developed on its lake. Sailing for pleasure and sport is very popular; it's a good guess that Skaneateles has more races and regattas than any other Finger Lake.

The most graceful time for lake travel was the steamboat era, roughly from the Civil War to World War I. Rail transportation—with dining cars—brought vacationers and wealthy cottagers to waiting boats on the shore of the Native Americans' "Long Water." Successors to those steamboats are operated today by Mid-Lakes Navigation. At 10 AM Monday through Saturday a boat leaves on one of the few remaining waterborne U.S. mail delivery routes. The mail boat serves cottagers around the lake, who wait on docks to snatch their mail from a long-handled fishing net. The kids at a summer camp down the lake are less passive—they usually paddle out in canoes. The mail cruise takes about three hours. For reservations, or information about other cruises, call 315-685-8500.

Bicycle Shops

M & R Sports, 286 Clark Street, Auburn (315-252-9069)

Nolan's Sporting Goods, 41 Genesee Street, Auburn (315-252-7249)

Restaurants

Bluewater Grill, 11 West Genesee Street, Skaneateles (315-685-6600)

Kabuki, 12 West Genesee Street, Skaneateles (315-685-7234)

Krebs, 53 West Genesee Street, Skaneateles (315-685-5714)

Sherwood Inn, 26 West Genesee Street, Skaneateles (315-685-3405)

—Updated by Steve Simpson

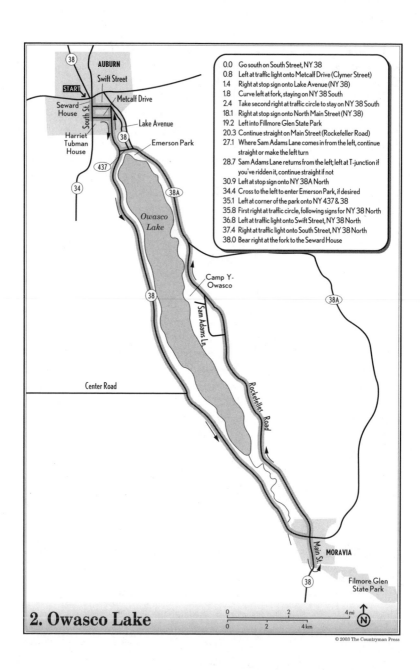

AUBURN
Swift Street

START

Seward House

South St.

Metcalf Drive

Lake Avenue

Harriet Tubman House

38

437

Emerson Park

34

38A

Owasco Lake

Camp Y-Owasco

Sam Adams Ln.

38

Center Road

Rockefeller Road

38A

MORAVIA

Main St.

38

Filmore Glen State Park

0.0   Go south on South Street, NY 38
0.8   Left at traffic light onto Metcalf Drive (Clymer Street)
1.4   Right at stop sign onto Lake Avenue (NY 38)
1.8   Curve left at fork, staying on NY 38 South
2.4   Take second right at traffic circle to stay on NY 38 South
18.1   Right at stop sign onto North Main Street (NY 38)
19.2   Left into Fillmore Glen State Park
20.3   Continue straight on Main Street (Rockefeller Road)
27.1   Where Sam Adams Lane comes in from the left, continue straight or make the left turn
28.7   Sam Adams Lane returns from the left; left at T-junction if you've ridden it, continue straight if not
30.9   Left at stop sign onto NY 38A North
34.4   Cross to the left to enter Emerson Park, if desired
35.1   Left at corner of the park onto NY 437 & 38
35.8   First right at traffic circle, following signs for NY 38 North
36.8   Left at traffic light onto Swift Street, NY 38 North
37.4   Right at traffic light onto South Street, NY 38 North
38.0   Bear right at the fork to the Seward House

0   2   4 mi
0   2   4 km

N

2. Owasco Lake

Owasco Lake

- **DISTANCE:** 38 miles; easy to moderate cycling
- **TERRAIN:** Some level riding with gradual hills
- **COUNTY MAP:** Cayuga

A day spent circling Owasco Lake can make one believe that the lake was created especially for cyclists. Eleven-mile-long Owasco, shortest of the six major Finger Lakes, provides a sparkling backdrop throughout most of your day, yet it is short enough to leave you time to enjoy the beautiful parks at each end of the lake. Both Fillmore Glen State Park, south of the lake, and Emerson Park at its foot have excellent swimming and picnicking facilities. The state park has secluded hiking trails and rural camping, while amenities at the county-run park near the city of Auburn include a theater, museums, and a dance pavilion. Ideal as well are the roads on either side of the lake, which gently lift you above the lake and then pleasantly roll you back down again.

Begin this tour at the Seward House on South Street in Auburn, just south of the Genesee Street shopping area. (To shorten this tour by about 6 miles, you can start at Emerson Park, on the north end of Owasco Lake, and ride to NY 38 South from there.)

0.0 Go south on South Street, NY 38.
Among the many fine old houses along Auburn's historic South Street is the William H. Seward House, a beautifully maintained memorial to the city's most famous son. The original house was built in 1817 by Judge Elijah Miller; Seward was permitted to marry the judge's 19-year-old daughter in 1824 after he agreed to move into the

Miller home. Through renovations and additions made from 1840 to 1870, the small late-Georgian residence grew into a 30-room mansion in the "Anglo-Italian" style. During these years Seward went on to become state senator, governor, and finally secretary of state under Lincoln and Johnson—when he made his name with the purchase of Alaska. Visitors to this remarkable home can inspect all three floors and see the transition from Federal home to Victorian mansion. All the furnishings belonged to the Seward family, the house's only occupants; clothing on display reveals that the most famous Seward was quite a diminutive fellow. The house is open Tuesday through Saturday, 1–4 PM, April through December. Admission of $4. includes a narrated tour through 16 rooms.

Other prominent Auburnians include William Burroughs, inventor of the adding machine; author and screenwriter Samuel Hopkins Adams; William Fargo, of the Wells-Fargo Express Company; architect Julius Schweinfurth; and Theodore Willard Case, cofounder of the Twentieth Century–Fox film studio. The Greek Revival mansion where Case developed the AEO bulb, permitting the recording of sound on film, is now the Cayuga Museum of History and Art, open Tuesday through Friday, 10 AM–5 PM. Next door is the attractive Schweinfurth Memorial Art Center (1981) with changing exhibits, open Tuesday through Saturday, 10 AM–5 PM and Sunday, 1–5 PM. For more information, call 315-255-1553.

Auburn is well supplied with restaurants and food stores, including a Wegmans Supermarket at the corner of Genesee and Osborne Streets. Halfway through the tour, the village of Moravia has a restaurant, food stores, and a take-out shop.

0.8 Turn left at the traffic light onto Metcalf Drive, also called Clymer Street. To see the onetime home of Harriet Tubman, don't turn left here but continue straight for about 0.4 mile; the house is on the left at 180 South Street Road. Built on land purchased from William Seward in 1857, the home was used as a refuge for slaves fleeing the South via the Underground Railroad. With a fearlessness that amazed her contemporaries, Tubman, called "the Moses of her people," led more than three hundred slaves from bondage. The home can be visited Tuesday through Friday 10 AM–4 PM or by appointment. Call 315-252-2081 for more information.

1.4 Turn right at the stop sign onto Lake Avenue (NY 38).

1.8 Curve left at the fork, staying on NY 38 South down the hill past the high school.

2.4 Take the second right at the traffic circle, to stay on NY 38 South.

In about 5 miles, note the fine 1835 cobblestone house on the right. Cobbles for this type of masonry were brought from the Lake Ontario plain.

By the time you reach Center Road, the gentle rise of NY 38, which has given you fine views of Owasco Lake, changes to a gradual descent. One large and several small cascades adorn the slope on your right; as you glide downhill you'll have a clear view of the lakehead marshland that is slowly encroaching on the lake.

18.1 Turn right at the stop sign onto North Main Street (NY 38).

Like Auburn, Moravia has had several notables, among them Jethro Wood, inventor of the cast-iron plow, and Millard Fillmore. Fillmore's rather uneventful presidency is commemorated in his native village by an annual bathtub race, said to be in honor of his improvements to the White House plumbing. Contestants in the late-July race can either contrive their own wheeled vessel or make use of a Rent-a-Tub program.

Just off Main Street is St. Matthew's Episcopal Church, whose chancel contains wood carvings by Oberammergau artist Hans Meyer.

19.2 Turn left into Fillmore Glen State Park.

Near the entrance is a reconstruction of the tiny log cabin in which Millard Fillmore was born in 1800. The park's magnificent gorge was carved by Fillmore Creek, which cut its way through layers of limestone and shale, creating five waterfalls and picturesque rock formations. Eight bridges along the gorge trail cross the creek, giving exceptional views of the glen. A stream-fed swimming area has been constructed at the lower end of the gorge, with a bathhouse, pavilion, tables, and fireplaces nearby. Campsites and cabins are also available. For more information, call 315-497-0130.

Leaving the park, turn right onto NY 38 North and retrace your route through the village of Moravia.

20.3 Continue straight, north, on Main Street, which becomes Rockefeller Road after leaving the village.

A little more than 3 miles farther is a sign marking the site of John D. Rockefeller's boyhood home. Here, Rockefeller later claimed, he raised wild turkeys for pocket money. John D.'s father, William, usually away from home peddling patent medicines and other questionable merchandise, often returned with handsome horses and generous gifts of money for his children. Some Moravians say horse thievery was one of his sidelines, though the claim has not been proved. Indicted in 1849 for the rape of a hired girl, the father's appearances became more rare, and he soon

SALLY WALTERS

In Auburn, the Cayuga Museum of History and Art displays early bicycles that make one grateful for their modern successors.

moved his family out of the county. Today the old Rockefeller house, on private land about a mile back from the road, has decayed nearly to ground level, evidently not a relic later generations of Rockefellers were eager to preserve. Local people report the remains of a tunnel through which the elder Rockefeller was said to have escaped from a posse pursuing horse thieves.

27.1 Where Sam Adams Lane comes in from the left, you can continue straight or make the left turn.
Both options give splendid views of the lake and well-kept farmland. Along Sam Adams Lane you'll pass the sign to Camp Y-Owasco, a lakeside recreation area that has 30 bunks in tents for American Youth Hostel members at a nominal charge. Swimming, meals, and tent camping are also available (315-253-5304). Open from the end of June through August.

28.7 Sam Adams Lane returns from the left. If you have ridden it, turn left at the T-junction; if not, continue straight.

30.9 Turn left at the stop sign onto NY 38A North.

34.4 Many cyclists will want to cross to the left along this stretch, to enter Emerson Park.
One of the most entertaining and well-maintained parks in the Finger Lakes, Emerson Park has carefully tended lawns and a wide beach excellent for picnicking and swimming. There are also snack bars, an imaginative playground, and the Merry-Go-Round Playhouse, presenting musicals throughout the summer (315-255-1305).

Across from the park's main entrance is the Agricultural Museum, open every afternoon, 11 AM–4 PM, May through October. Exhibited are many products of the local farm-equipment manufacturers who united to form International Harvester.

35.1 Turn left at the corner of the park onto NY 437 and 38.

35.8 Take the first right at the traffic circle, following signs for NY 38 North and the city of Auburn.

36.8 Turn left at the traffic light onto Swift Street, NY 38 North.

37.4 Turn right at the traffic light onto South Street, NY 38 North.

38.0 Bearing right at the fork will take you to the Seward House, where the tour began.

Those wishing to spend the night in Auburn will find a reasonably priced Days Inn adjacent to the Seward House.

Bicycle Shops

M & R Sports, 286 Clark Street, Auburn (315-252-9069)

Mike's Bikes, Boards and Bows, 360 Grant Avenue, Auburn (315-253-0585)

Nolan's Sporting Goods, 41 Genesee Street, Auburn (315-252-7249)

For More Information

Cayuga County Office of Tourism (1-800-499-9615)

—Updated by Jeff Page

3

Finger Lakes Heartland:
A Three-Day Tour

- **DISTANCE:** 115 miles
- **TERRAIN:** Cycling difficulty and terrain are given for each day
- **COUNTY MAPS:** Cayuga, Schuyler, Seneca, Tompkins

Seneca and Cayuga, the longest, widest, and deepest of the Finger Lakes, lie at the heart of this region. Both occupy glacier-enlarged valleys, and both have bottoms below sea level. In song, Cornell University hails its scenic location "far above Cayuga's waters"; in fact it shares this distinction with Wells and Ithaca Colleges, while above Seneca Lake sit Hobart and William Smith Colleges. All these schools can be visited on this tour, along with a winery, several museums, and the Women's Rights National Historical Park in Seneca Falls, birthplace of the American women's rights movement. The city of Ithaca has many excellent restaurants serving the greatest variety of food in the Finger Lakes. And for rural pleasures, this route passes some of the most scenic state parks in the area.

Most riders will want to devote three days to this tour. Fast riders can cut it down to two, while those with more time may want to spend a week or so on the circuit. The days are planned for riders seeking indoor overnight accommodations (see the end of this tour for lodging information and suggestions). The tour begins in Geneva with a long first day to Ithaca; both cities have a selection of motels and guest houses. The second day is shorter and easier, ending at Aurora, where there is an excellent old inn; and the third

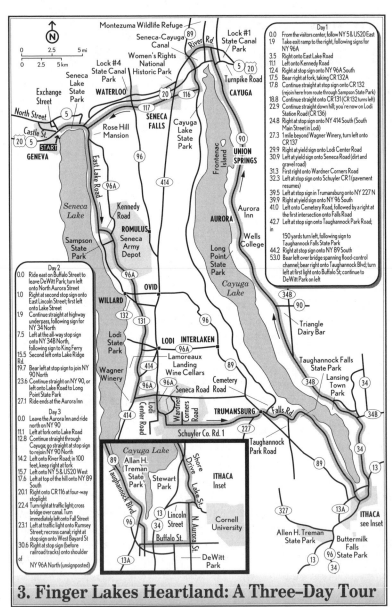

3. Finger Lakes Heartland: A Three-Day Tour

day returns you to your starting point in Geneva in a little more than 30 miles.

Campers have greater flexibility. Both lakes are well served by excellent state parks and some private campgrounds, so there is no need to keep to the daily schedules outlined below. The state parks along the route that permit camping include Sampson, Taughannock Falls, Buttermilk Falls, Robert Treman, Long Point, and Cayuga Lake. Reservations for overnight stays are recommended, particularly on summer weekends. These may be made 2 days to 11 months ahead by calling 1-800-456-CAMP. While the route is the same for campers and noncampers, riders with tents can bypass Geneva. Directions for this shortcut are given in the tour.

DAY ONE

54 miles; moderate to strenuous cycling
Rolling terrain with one steep hill

This tour starts at the visitors center, Geneva Area Chamber of Commerce, at the corner of Lakefront Drive (NY 5 and US 20) and Lake Street. Overnight parking is not allowed here but may be arranged at the Geneva Recreation Complex about 0.25 mile west on South Exchange Street (call for availability: 315-789-5005). Parking may also be available for those who stay at the Ramada Inn on the waterfront, adjacent to the visitors center, before or after the tour (315-789-0400). Or you can make other arrangements with the various motels and guesthouses nearby; see the list at the end of this tour. Because there are limited food sources until you reach Trumansburg (40 miles from Geneva), you should bring food and water with you. The Geneva area is well supplied with grocery stores.

0.0 From the visitors center at the corner of Lake Street and Lakefront Drive (NY 5 and US 20), follow NY 5 and US 20 East—with the lake on your right. *As you ride, Seneca Lake State Park, with swimming and picnicking facilities, is between the highway and the lake. The paved lakeside pathways look inviting, but unfortunately there is no exit at the park's east end.*

1.9 Take the exit ramp to the right, following signs for NY 96A and Ovid and Ithaca.

After you cross the bridge, the first right turn, onto Boody Hill's Road, leads to a good seafood restaurant, the Crow's Nest. Across an inlet from the Seneca Lake State Park Marina, the restaurant's spacious terrace and airy dining room afford pleasant lake vistas.

Soon after Boody Hill's Road you'll see Rose Hill (1839) on the left, one of the finest Greek Revival houses in the country. The mansion has been exquisitely restored, complete with the Empire furnishings popular from 1820 to 1840 (look for the characteristic claw foot). Admission is $3 for adults, $2 for senior citizens and students 10–18 years old; children under 10—no charge. The house is open daily May through October, Monday through Saturday 10 AM–4 PM and Sunday 1–5 PM.

3.5 Turn right onto East Lake Road.

11.1 Turn left onto Kennedy Road.

12.4 Turn right at the stop sign onto NY 96A South.

The highway gets moderate traffic but has a wide, often paved, shoulder.

In a mile and a half you'll reach Sampson State Park. Campers may want to spend the night, or to start their tour here. The park was opened by the state in 1960 on what was once the huge Sampson naval base. During World War II, Sampson was the second largest training facility in the country, with more than forty thousand men housed here. Forty-one of the Navy's 208 buildings remain, as well as an extensive network of roads, most now closed to motorized traffic but open to cyclists.

If you explore the park, or use its swimming or camping facilities, you may want to continue to Willard without going back to NY 96A. To do this, take the park's entrance road to the T-junction (past the circle) and turn left (south). You'll pass the maintenance garage, which was once the base firehouse. Here cycle past the barrier that says SERVICE ROAD—DO NOT ENTER. Thereafter, go right at all forks. You'll have an empty lakeside road all the way to the barrier marking the former boundary of the base. Beyond the barrier, the road continues along the shore, then curves left to bring you to Willard, where you rejoin the described route by turning right onto CR 132.

17.5 Bear right at the fork, taking CR 132A and following the sign to Willard.

Rose Hill, just east of Geneva, is considered one of the finest Greek Revival homes in the country.

17.8 Continue straight at the stop sign onto CR 132. (If you chose the route through Sampson State Park, this is where you rejoin the tour.)
Behind the fence on your right is the Willard Drug Treatment Campus, created in 1995 for minor drug offenders. For over a century this was the Willard Psychiatric Center, and was originally built in the 1860s as the New York State Agricultural College. After the Civil War, the college was moved to Ithaca, where it became part of Cornell University.

18.8 Continue straight onto CR 131, as CR 132 turns left.
In about 4 miles you'll pass a right turn for Lodi State Park, a secluded lakeside picnic area with bathhouses and boat-launching facilities.

22.9 Continue straight down the hill. You are now on Lodi Station Road, or CR 136, which curves left past a cemetery toward Lodi.

24.8 Turn right at the stop sign onto NY 414 South (South Main Street in the town of Lodi).

In about 3 miles you'll see the Lamoreaux Landing Wine Cellars on your right, followed in 0.25 mile by the Wagner Winery and Microbrewery. Here shaded picnic tables near a small pond and the terrace of the Ginny Lee Café provide a picturesque setting from which to enjoy a splendid view over the vineyards to Seneca Lake. The café is open daily 11 AM–4 PM. Wagner's wine and beer production is small, and its quality is very high.

27.3 About 1 mile beyond the Wagner Winery, turn left onto CR 137, and begin a stiff climb of just less than 2 miles.

When General Sullivan's Colonial army passed this way on September 3, 1779, a soldier entered in his diary: "This day we passed over a fine Beautiful country of land adjoining Seneca Lake on the west and the Cayuga Lake on the east." The soldiers were not just sight-seeing; they had been promised land once the war ended. Three years after the Sullivan campaign, the Military Tract was created; 600 acres went to privates, and more to officers. Some men settled on their land, and many more sold to speculators. The township lines in the 1.5-million-acre tract were drawn with a ruler, ignoring topography. Many roads here retain the original grid pattern, forming almost mile-square boxes, representing a private's bounty. The 28 townships in the tract were given classical names; on this tour you'll ride through Junius, Romulus, Ovid, Hector, Ulysses, Milton, Scipio, and Aurelius.

29.9 Turn right at the yield sign onto Lodi Center Road.

30.9 Turn left at the yield sign onto Seneca Road. For the next 1.4 miles the surface is well-graded packed dirt and gravel.

31.3 Turn at the first right onto Wardner Corners Road.

32.3 Turn left at the stop sign onto Schuyler CR 1, where pavement resumes. *You'll see signs for the Finger Lakes National Forest and its rustic Blueberry Patch Campground (see Tour 17 for details). Soon you'll pass the crest of the ridge between the lakes and roll easily toward Cayuga Lake.*

39.5 Turn left at the stop sign in Trumansburg onto NY 227 North.

39.9 Turn right at the yield sign onto NY 96 South.

When Revolutionary War soldier Abner Treman drew for his share of the military tract, he got lot #2 of township 22 (Ulysses), a strip of land 0.75 mile by 2 miles in which the village of Trumansburg is now located. The village was originally named Treman's Village; a post office error around 1814 accounts for the present spelling.

Trumansburg has several supermarkets and small good restaurants—the influence of Cornell University in nearby Ithaca is already evident. As you leave the village you'll pass a sign on your right for the Podunk Ski Center, which also operates as a youth hostel. For information on this and other Finger Lakes hostels, write to AYH, 459 Westcott Street, Syracuse, NY 13210.

41.0 About 0.25 mile past the school (on the right), turn left onto Cemetery Road, followed by a right at the first intersection onto Falls Road. (The cemetery should be on your left.)

42.7 Turn left at the stop sign onto Taughannock Park Road; in 150 yards turn left, following the sign to Taughannock Falls State Park.
Two-thirds of the way down the long hill through the park is the headquarters of the Finger Lakes State Parks Commission, where information on all the region's parks can be obtained.

Campers may want to spend the night here, as reaching the two state parks just past Ithaca requires some uncomfortable highway riding. The park's hiking trails lead to scenic lookouts over the stream-carved gorge and 215-foot Taughannock Falls.

44.2 Turn right at the stop sign onto NY 89 South.
NY 89 is narrow, with little or no shoulder, short sight distances, and sometimes fast traffic. It must be endured, if not enjoyed.

53.0 After passing the Allan Treman State Marine Park and the municipal park, bear left over the bridge spanning the flood-control channel. Bear right onto Taughannock Boulevard and turn left at the first light onto Buffalo Street. Continue several blocks to DeWitt Park, on your left.

54.0 This day's ride ends at DeWitt Park, a convenient central location adjacent to Buffalo and Cayuga Streets.
The delights of Ithaca more than make up for its less-than-ideal traffic conditions. Those who choose to spend the night near town have options ranging from the growing number of bed-and-breakfast establishments listed in brochures to the Ramada Inn. Campers have a choice of Robert Treman or Buttermilk Falls State Parks, reached via busy NY 13 South. Both parks encompass spectacular glens several miles long with numerous waterfalls. They are dazzling spectacles, as well as convenient places to picnic or to swim in stream-fed gorge pools.

Thanks to Cornell, Ithaca is a small city with an artsy, cosmopolitan atmosphere;

on and off campus, culture and natural beauty blend nicely—Ithaca well deserves its classical name. This ideal situation has only one flaw for cyclists: Just about everything in this precipitous city is up or down a very long, steep hill. Once you get up to Cornell, plan to stay there for a while. A map of the Cornell campus is available in the student union building, Willard Straight Hall, where you can also check the calendar of events. You'll find attractions from agriculture to fine arts: films, concerts, lectures, an art museum, and architectural tours of the campus (given weekly in summer). The 2,600-acre arboretum, Cornell Plantations, has miles of winding trails east of the main campus, and the well-known Laboratory of Ornithology is a couple of miles northeast, off NY 13 North, on Sapsucker Woods Road. The central campus, overlooking city and lake and bordered by two striking gorges, is perhaps the most beautiful in the country.

DeWitt Park is named for Simeon DeWitt, who laid out the townships in the military tract. Across from the park is the DeWitt Mall, small shops and restaurants in a former school. Another example of skillful urban renewal is the Ithaca Commons, a pedestrian shopping mall in the heart of the city.

Ithaca is a diner's paradise, with restaurants for every budget and taste. Turback's, in an 1852 Victorian Gothic farmhouse near the state parks on NY 13 South, has a salad bar so complete—from breads and soup to make-your-own ice cream sundaes—that the fine entrées are almost superfluous. In the summer, area wineries offer free samples in Turback's book-lined bar. Among Ithaca's excellent vegetarian restaurants are The Cabbagetown Café on Eddy Street (near the Cornell campus) and Moosewood (in the DeWitt Mall).

DAY TWO

27 miles; moderate cycling

Rolling terrain with one long, gradual hill

There are a few grocery stores and restaurants along today's route, but it may be more convenient to stop at any of Ithaca's numerous bakeries and delis for food to carry with you.

0.0 Leave DeWitt Park by riding east on Buffalo Street (the park will be on your left); in 0.2 mile, turn left just before the hill, onto North Aurora Street.

1.0 Turn right at the second stop sign onto East Lincoln Street; then take the first left onto Lake Street. Soon you'll cross a bridge with Ithaca Falls to your right.

1.9 At the highway underpass, continue straight, following the sign for NY 34 North.

Making the first left after the underpass will bring you to Stewart Park, featuring a small zoo, a merry-go-round, tennis courts, and picnic facilities. Fishing is allowed (swimming is not), and a concession rents canoes, rowboats, and sailboats. Immediately beyond the park turnoff is the Tompkins County Visitor Center. The route out of Ithaca is marked by gradual uphills, with more than 3 miles of climbing in the first 7.

7.5 Turn left at the all-way stop sign onto NY 34B North, following the sign to King Ferry.

After this turn, past the 1830 brick tavern called Rogue's Harbor, there is a long downhill followed by a long uphill. Before the uphill, a turn to the left on Myers Road just before the All Saints Church will take you to Lansing Town Park, with opportunities for fishing, swimming, and picnicking.

15.5 From NY 34B North, take the second left onto narrow Lake Ridge Road. This turn is not conspicuous; it comes after a short rise and is opposite an old cemetery.

19.7 At the stop sign, bear left to join NY 90 North.

The Triangle Dairy Bar at this intersection is locally popular for good, simple country fare, ice cream, and homemade desserts. The King Ferry Hotel is located 1 mile east of this intersection (315-364-5124).

23.6 Continue straight on NY 90, or turn left onto Lake Road to visit Long Point State Park.

This peaceful boaters park has a rustic campground; along the lake is a picnic area where a sign prohibiting swimming is generally ignored. Both NY 90 and Lake Road lead to Aurora.

27.1 This day's ride ends at the Aurora Inn.

The village of Aurora was named earlier just as appealingly by Native Americans, who called their settlement here Deawendote or "Village of Constant Dawn." This college town along a half-moon cove of Cayuga Lake fulfills whatever expectations its attractive names suggest. Twenty-six-year-old Henry Wells first saw Aurora in 1832 when he fetched a shipment of wheat from the old steam mill (still standing behind the Aurora Inn). In 1850 he moved to town permanently, and the same year he became president of the American Express Company, having earlier formed, with William Fargo, the famous company linking their names. Wells College, a four-year women's liberal-arts school, was founded by its benefactor in 1868. Wells's large, graceful, limestone home, Glen Park (1852), is now one of the college buildings, set amid wide lawns under tall shade trees.

Under several names and serving various functions (including college dormitory), the Aurora Inn has been a village landmark since 1833. It is owned by Wells College (as are many of the best old buildings) and operated by the Aurora Foundation. The inn underwent a multimillion-dollar renovation in 2003 and reopened as a remarkable destination with imaginative decor and food, impeccable interiors, sweeping lawns and gardens, quiet comfort, and noteworthy service. The restaurant, which overlooks the lake, offers breakfast, lunch, and dinner, all moderately priced, and using fresh local ingredients. Guest rooms (many with fireplaces and balconies) range from $125 to $225 for two. Call ahead for reservations, as this is the only lodging in town (315-364-8888). Surrounding the inn are more dining options: Pizzaurora offers subs and pizza, Fargo serves tavern fare, and Dori's has ice cream that shouldn't be missed. To explore the village further, follow the walking-tour guide for sale at Jane Morgan's Little House on Main Street.

DAY THREE

33.5 miles; easy to moderate cycling

Mostly level with some rolling terrain

There's a small grocery store in Aurora and opportunities to shop or dine throughout today's ride.

0.0 Leave the Aurora Inn, riding north on NY 90 (the lake will be on your left).
In Oak Glen Cemetery on the north edge of the village is the grave of Henry Wells. Four miles farther, on the right, is a marker on the site of the capital of the Cayuga Indians, destroyed by Sullivan's army in 1779.

One mile north of Aurora is the main manufacturing plant of MacKenzie-Childs, a manufacturer, wholesaler, and retailer of decorated pottery, linens, footstools, and other home furnishings. There is a very nice restaurant on site, though reservations are required (315-364-9688). Studio tours are available ($10 for adults) Monday–Friday at 1:15 PM (1-877-711-3922).

Union Springs, about 6 miles north of Aurora, has food stores and prepared meals. In the lake, opposite the village, is Frontenac Island, one of two islands in the Finger Lakes and the site of an early Native American burial ground that has yielded rich archaeological remains.

11.1 Turn left at the fork onto Lake Road.
Before construction of the Erie Canal, 40-mile-long Cayuga Lake and the extensive marshlands to its north were serious obstacles to east–west transport. The wooden Cayuga Bridge, completed in 1800, was one of the marvels of its day, spanning a mile of lake between Cayuga Village and Bridgeport. Timothy Dwight, a president of Yale, was suitably impressed when he saw it in 1804: "The bridge . . . may be justly styled a stupendous erection; . . . probably the longest work of the kind in the United States. . . . The toll is a quarter of a dollar for man and horse; the highest, I believe, in the United States." In the 1850s, the bridge was allowed to deteriorate.

12.8 Continue straight through Cayuga, past the sprawling buildings of the former Beacon Feed Company. Go straight at the stop sign to rejoin NY 90 North.

14.2 Turn left onto River Road, where Turnpike Road enters from the right. In 100 feet, keep right at the fork.
You'll pass the trim park and picnic area at Lock #1 of the Cayuga and Seneca Canal, which links the lakes with the Barge Canal.

15.7 Turn left onto NY 5 and US 20 West.
Shortly after crossing the canal on the bridge dedicated to French missionary Rene Menard, you'll see the entrance to the Montezuma Wildlife Refuge on your right. Details on the refuge can be found in Tour 15.

17.6 Turn left at the top of the hill onto NY 89 South.

20.1 Turn right onto CR 116 at a four-way stoplight.
The campus of the New York State Chiropractic College (formerly Eisenhower College) is at this corner. If you continue south on NY 89 instead of making the right turn, you'll reach Cayuga Lake State Park in about a mile. This beautiful 186-acre park has a beach, a picnic area, pavilions, hiking trails, 14 cabins, and nearly 300 campsites.

CR 116 becomes East Bayard Street at the Seneca Falls village limits. Shortly after the cemetery, Washington Street, on your right, marks the eastern boundary of the Women's Rights National Historical Park, operated by the National Park

Service. If you turn right onto Washington, you'll reach the Elizabeth Cady Stanton House in 0.2 mile. The talented and prolific women's-rights pioneer lived here with her husband and numerous children from 1847 to 1862. Van Cleef Lake, down the hill from the house, had not been created at that time; residents on this side could walk from island to island, amid mills and rapids, to the village center. Tours of the restored Stanton house are conducted June through September by the Park Service.

Continuing straight on East Bayard, you'll see the Amelia Jenks Bloomer House on the right at number 53, near the junction with Washington Street. Mrs. Bloomer was active in the temperance movement, editing the society's newspaper, The Lily. She did not invent the costume that was named after her; Elizabeth Smith Miller, a cousin of Mrs. Stanton, introduced the garment to Geneva, New York, after having seen it worn by ladies in Swiss sanitariums.

22.4 Turn right at the traffic light and cross the bridge over the Cayuga and Seneca Canal. Then turn left immediately after the bridge onto Fall Street, Seneca Falls's main street.

At the time of the first Women's Rights Convention in 1848, Seneca Falls was a bustling mill and manufacturing town situated along the Seneca Turnpike (now Fall Street) and a feeder canal of the Erie. When Elizabeth Cady Stanton moved here from Boston, where she had been active in the abolitionist movement, she found life in this small working-class town painfully restricted. "I suffered with mental hunger," she wrote, "which, like an empty stomach, is very depressive."

Joining with four other women, some from the liberal Quaker community in nearby Waterloo, Stanton called the first Women's Rights Convention on July 19 and 20, 1848, in the local Wesleyan Chapel. Here was drafted the radical Declaration of Sentiments and Resolutions, which insisted that women "have immediate admission to all the rights and privileges which belong to them as citizens of the United States." Embellished by the speeches of well-known abolitionists Lucretia Mott and Frederick Douglass, the convention drew more than three hundred people and the attention of national newspapers, which published the declaration alongside indignant editorials. Such notice added to the success of the convention, even though many supporters refused to sign the landmark document because it demanded women's suffrage.

The Park Service Visitor Center on Fall Street (open daily 9 AM–5 PM) near the former chapel has historical displays and information on park tours and activities. More exhibits on women's history, both local and national, are found at the

Women's Hall of Fame on Fall Street, open year-round 10 AM–4 PM Monday through Saturday, and from May through September 12–4 PM on Sunday. Admission is $3 for adults.

The recently refurbished turn-of-the-20th-century Gould Hotel, in the village center, has fine cuisine and a limited number of guest rooms. Standard motels are common along busy NY 5 and US 20 between here and Geneva, 12 miles west.

23.1 Turn left at the traffic light onto Rumsey Street and recross the canal; in 0.2 mile, turn right at the stop sign onto West Bayard Street.

In about 3 miles those wishing to go into Waterloo for groceries or to find lodgings in motels along NY 5 and US 20 can turn right onto Washington Street, where you'll cross the canal again and pass the canal park at Lock #4. Two houses of the Women's Rights Park are here, those of Jane Hunt (401 East Main Street) and Mary Ann McClintock (16 East Williams Street), who helped organize the convention of 1848.

To bypass Waterloo, continue straight on West Bayard.

30.6 Turn right at the stop sign (before the railroad tracks) onto the shoulder of NY 96A North (unsignposted). Campers headed for Sampson State Park can bypass Geneva by turning left here. You'll soon see the Rose Hill mansion on the left, and you can pick up the tour directions at that point.

31.2 Ride to the left at the fork, following signs to Geneva and NY 5 and US 20 West.

Riding these 2 miles of busy highway is unpleasant but unavoidable. In a short time you'll return to where this tour began 115 miles before.

For information on the history and sites of Geneva, see Tour 4.

Nearby Accommodations

Archway B&B, 7020 Searsburg Road, Trumansburg (607-387-6175)

Buttermilk Falls B&B, 110 East Buttermilk Falls Road, Ithaca (607-272-6767)

Chamberlain Mansion Inn, 30 Cayuga Street, Seneca Falls (315-568-9990)

Gothic Eves B&B, 112 East Main Street, Trumansburg (1-800-387-7712)

Hanshaw House, 15 Sapsucker Woods Road, Ithaca (607-257-1437)

Log Country Inn, 4 La Rue Road, Ithaca (607-589-4771)

Podunk Ski Center Youth Hostel, c/o AYH, 459 Wescott Street, Syracuse 13210

Ramada Inn—Geneva Lakefront, NY 5 and US 20, Geneva (315-789-0400)

Ramada Inn Ithaca Airport, 2310 North Triphammer Road, Ithaca (607-257-3100)

Bicycle Shops

The Bike Rack, 414 College Avenue, Ithaca (607-272-1010)

Geneva Bicycle Center, 489 Exchange Street, Geneva (315-789-5922)

Pedal-Away, 111 South Fulton Street, Ithaca (607-272-5425)

For More Information

Geneva Area Chamber of Commerce, 32 Lakefront Drive, P.O. Box 587, Geneva 14456 (315-789-1776)

Ithaca/Tompkins County Convention and Visitors Bureau, 904 East Shore Drive, Ithaca (607-272-1313; 1-800-284-8422)

—Updated by Brendan Brady

4

Geneva–Phelps–Gorham

- **DISTANCE:** 37 miles; easy cycling
- **TERRAIN:** Level terrain with very gently rolling hills
- **COUNTY MAP:** Ontario

To see rural farming landscapes that are close to kids' picture-book idealizations, take a ride through Ontario County. Farmhouses are old and well kept, hedgerows and fences in good repair, woodlots healthy. More than a third of county farm income is from dairying, with the next largest amount coming from vegetable growing. The county ranks first in the nation in production of table beets and cabbage for sauerkraut, and it leads the state in wheat production. Other common crops include oats, rye, and barley; alfalfa and other hay crops; feed corn, beans, and fruits.

Places of cultural or historical interest are numerous on this tour, especially in and around the city of Geneva, where you start and finish. Geneva is old—the first settled city west of Albany. Its South Main Street, laid out in 1796, has been called "the most beautiful old Colonial thoroughfare outside New England." To the frontier its large homes and quaint rowhouses brought an air of East Coast urbanity. Roads throughout this route get very little traffic—even on weekends in summer. The urban riding is interesting, and the rural riding delightful.

The ride starts on Geneva's South Main Street, at the campus of Hobart and William Smith Colleges.

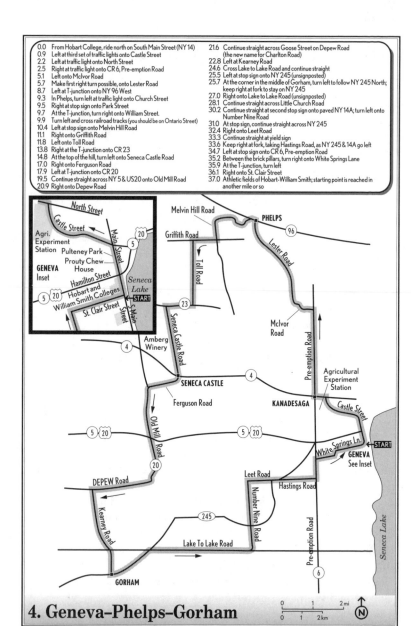

0.0 From Hobart College, ride north on South Main Street (NY 14)
0.9 Left at third set of traffic lights onto Castle Street
2.2 Left at traffic light onto North Street
2.5 Right at traffic light onto CR 6, Pre-emption Road
5.1 Left onto McIvor Road
5.7 Make first right turn possible, onto Lester Road
8.7 Left at T-junction onto NY 96 West
9.3 In Phelps, turn left at traffic light onto Church Street
9.5 Right at stop sign onto Park Street
9.7 At the T-junction, turn right onto William Street.
9.9 Turn left and cross railroad tracks (you should be on Ontario Street)
10.4 Left at stop sign onto Melvin Hill Road
11.1 Right onto Griffith Road
11.8 Left onto Toll Road
13.8 Right at the T-junction onto CR 23
14.8 At the top of the hill, turn left onto Seneca Castle Road
17.0 Right onto Ferguson Road
17.9 Left at T-junction onto CR 20
19.5 Continue straight across NY 5 & US20 onto Old Mill Road
20.9 Right onto Depew Road

21.6 Continue straight across Goose Street on Depew Road (the new name for Charlton Road)
22.8 Left at Kearney Road
24.6 Cross Lake to Lake Road and continue straight
25.5 Left at stop sign onto NY 245 (unsignposted)
25.7 At the corner in the middle of Gorham, turn left to follow NY 245 North; keep right at fork to stay on NY 245
27.0 Right onto Lake to Lake Road (unsignposted)
28.1 Continue straight across Little Church Road
30.2 Continue straight at second stop sign onto paved NY 14A; turn left onto Number Nine Road
31.0 At stop sign, continue straight across NY 245
32.4 Right onto Leet Road
33.3 Continue straight at yield sign
33.6 Keep right at fork, taking Hastings Road, as NY 245 & 14A go left
34.7 Left at stop sign onto CR 6, Pre-emption Road
35.2 Between the brick pillars, turn right onto White Springs Lane
35.9 At the T-junction, turn left
36.1 Right onto St. Clair Street
37.0 Athletic fields of Hobart-William Smith; starting point is reached in another mile or so

4. Geneva–Phelps–Gorham

0   1   2 mi
0 1 2 km

N

0.0 From the Hobart College campus, ride north (with the lake to your right) on South Main Street, NY 14.

Geneva College was founded in 1822. Its name was changed in 1851 to honor its founder, Bishop John Henry Hobart. The oldest buildings, Geneva Hall and Trinity Hall, face both the college quadrangle and South Main Street. Hobart's associated women's college, William Smith, was founded in 1906.

A few of the impressive old houses along Main Street are college residences, but many more are still in private hands. Through the 19th century South Main Street maintained a decidedly genteel atmosphere, begun by transplanted southern gentry and continued by a disproportionate number of retired ministers and well-born spinsters. The Prouty-Chew House (1825) at 543 South Main Street can be visited Tuesday through Friday 9:30 AM–4:30 PM. Its furnishings reflect Federal through Victorian styles, and the lower floor is home to the Geneva Historical Society.

A hundred or so yards downhill from the Prouty-Chew House is Pulteney Park (where cattle grazed until 1862), laid out by Capt. Charles Williamson, agent for Sir William Pulteney and his English associates, who then owned much of western New York. Behind the park, the Pulteney Apartments contain some of the fabric of Williamson's 1796 Geneva Hotel, long a marvel of elegance. Williamson had hanging gardens planted on the precipice facing the lake and decreed that the east side of Main Street should not be built upon, so that hotel guests could have an unobstructed view of the lake. The rowhouses that did come after his time mitigate the loss of the lake view with their own charm.

On the right side of South Main Street a historical marker notes the place where Elizabeth Blackwell became the first woman to graduate from a medical school in America. The Geneva Medical College she attended was part of Hobart, which, of course, admitted only men. Faculty and students assumed Blackwell's application to be a joke, and it was accepted in that spirit. On arrival, she was advised to leave immediately; she refused, and in two years she had her medical degree. Dr. Blackwell soon founded the New York City Infirmary for Women and Children, and in time she received many honors, both in America and in her native England.

0.9 Turn left at the third set of traffic lights, onto Castle Street. Two left turns are possible at this corner; make the less sharp left, so that the Soldiers & Sailors (1834) library is to your right.

There are several restaurants and luncheonettes in Geneva, including, at this intersection, Wing Tai, one of the few Chinese restaurants in the Finger Lakes region.

You'll pass a small supermarket on Castle Street and will find other food stores and a restaurant or two in the villages along this route.

Just less than a mile along Castle Street a marker identifies the Smith Observatory of Dr. William R. Brooks, a self-taught 19th-century astronomer who discovered 27 comets, more than anyone else.

2.2 At the traffic light, turn left onto North Street.
To the right at this corner is a fine example of an octagon house, an original American style popular in the 1850s. The design's creator, phrenologist Orson Fowler, promised economy of materials, functional interiors, good views, and improved health of occupants.

The campuslike area to the left is part of the New York State Agricultural Experiment Station, a branch of the State University of New York and Cornell University. In 1882 the station began research to benefit New York's leading industry, agriculture. Emphasis is on fruit and vegetable experiments, with departments ranging from cytology to food technology. Six Geneva-developed apples are among the top 20 in the state; of these the best known are Empire, Cortland, and Macoun. There is a small public display area in the lobby of the Entomology and Plant Pathology Building.

2.5 Turn right at the traffic light onto CR 6, Pre-emption Road.
Past Conklins Corner Store, a sign on the left marks the site of Kanadesaga, where Sir William Johnson built a fort for England's Indian allies in 1756. The village was once the home of the Senecas' chief sachem. Behind the gas station a Native American burial mound can be discerned.

The Pre-emption line you are riding along, on CR 6, dates from a 1786 compromise between Massachusetts and New York, both claiming sovereignty over what is now western New York. The deal worked out gave New York sovereignty over the region but allowed Massachusetts preemptive rights to sell the land west of the line. Massachusetts quickly did sell, though the buyers were cheated somewhat by a surveying error (said to be deliberate).

CR 6 actually runs along what's called Old Pre-emption Line; the true line runs a couple of miles to the east. The narrow wedge between the lines was referred to as the Gore.

5.1 Turn left onto McIvor Road.

5.7 Make the first right turn possible, onto Lester Road.
Two miles farther, a sign marks the location of the Red House Observatory, where

The mill run at Lock #29 in Phelps, New York

Dr. William Brooks discovered 11 comets between 1881 and 1888, the year he moved to Geneva.

8.7 Turn left at the T-junction onto NY 96 West just past the Finger Lakes Road underpass.

The village of Phelps—which for some unknown reason was first called Woodpecker City—is named in honor of Oliver Phelps, who, with Nathaniel Gorham, purchased 2.6 million acres in 1788 from the state of Massachusetts almost all of what is now New York west of Seneca Lake. A sweetener in the deal, allowing Phelps and Gorham to pay in depreciated Massachusetts securities, turned sour when Alexander Hamilton led the federal government to assume the debts of the states. The value of Massachusetts notes skyrocketed. By 1790 Phelps and Gorham had failed to make payments, Gorham went bankrupt, and Massachusetts took back about two-thirds of the original purchase. Most of the remaining third (1.25 million acres) was sold by the partners to Robert Morris, the financier of the American Revolution and a friend of George Washington. In 1791 Morris sold at a profit to the English syndicate headed by Sir William Pulteney.

The Pulteney interests, led by their daring, dashing, and extravagant land agent, Scottish Capt. Charles Williamson, left the greatest mark on western New York's early development. But Oliver Phelps and Nathaniel Gorham opened in Canandaigua the first land office in America, and both gave their names to Ontario County villages.

9.3 In the village of Phelps, turn left at the traffic light onto Church Street.
A block along the left, the library has made wonderful use of an 1849 stone church designed by David Bates Douglass, an American polymath who also planned Brooklyn's Greenwood Cemetery and the New York City water supply system, surveyed part of the United States–Canadian border, taught mathematics at West Point and Hobart, and was president of Kenyon College.

The high point of the year in this cabbage town, home of the Silver Floss Kraut Company, is the Sauerkraut Festival, held in early August. Special features of the two-day event include the speed sauerkraut-eating contest and the cutting of the sauerkraut cake—with free pieces to the first one thousand takers.

9.5 Turn right at the stop sign onto Park Street.
Along this street is a shady village park.

9.7 At the T-junction, turn right onto William Street.

9.9 Turn left and cross the railroad tracks. You should now be on Ontario Street.

10.4 Turn left at the stop sign onto Melvin Hill Road.

11.1 Turn right onto Griffith Road.

11.8 Turn left onto Toll Road.
It seems surprising that a toll could have been charged on such a rural road, but in the early years of the 19th century the state lacked resources to serve its burgeoning western frontier, and private companies were licensed to build roads and turn a profit where they could.

13.8 At the T-junction, turn right onto CR 23.

14.8 At the top of the hill, turn left onto Seneca Castle Road.
The hill you just climbed brought you up the steep west side of a drumlin; riding south you enjoy a long, gentle downhill. On the right is the Amberg Winery.

In the hamlet of Seneca Castle, no turns are made. "Castle" does not signify a fortification; it was simply a term the Dutch and English colonists applied to Native

American villages, regardless of their military usefulness.

Not too long ago, in late summer and autumn you would have seen—and on warm days smelled—cabbages in fields or at roadside stands. Years ago, work crews had to load 10-pound cabbages into trucks with long pitchforks, surely one of the toughest of harvest chores. Later, a Seneca Castle man developed a mechanical cabbage picker, which was manufactured there.

17.0 Just as houses yield to farmland, turn right onto Ferguson Road.

17.9 Turn left at the T-junction, onto CR 20. (Old Mill Road).

19.5 Continue straight across NY 5 and US 20 onto Old Mill Road.
Along Flint Creek we have seen wild turkeys. They are slimmer than the domesticated variety and move quickly through the underbrush. The best chance to see the birds is in early spring, before leaves are fully out.

20.9 Just past Frog Hollow, turn right onto Charlton Road.

21.6 Continue straight across Goose Street on Depew Road (the new name for Charlton Road).

22.8 Turn left at Kearney Road.

24.6 Cross Lake to Lake Road and continue straight.

25.5 Turn left at the stop sign onto NY 245 (unsignposted).

25.7 At the corner in the middle of Gorham, turn left to follow NY 245 North. At the fork, keep right to stay on NY 245.

27.0 Turn right onto Lake to Lake Road (unsignposted).

28.1 Continue straight across Little Church Road.

30.2 At the second stop sign, continue straight onto the paved NY 14A. In about 150 yards, turn left onto Number Nine Road.
The unusual name of this road dates from the survey of the Phelps-Gorham Purchase of 1788, when townships had only numbers.

31.0 At the stop sign, continue straight across NY 245.

32.4 Turn right onto Leet Road.

33.3 Continue straight at the yield sign.

33.6 Keep right at the fork, taking Hastings Road, as NY 245 and 14A go left. *If you are traveling between August and October, you will shortly see acres of dahlias to the right. Legg Dahlia Gardens is one of the 50 or so nurseries for which Geneva was once famous. Visitors are welcome daily 8 AM–sunset; admission is free.*

34.7 Turn left at the stop sign onto CR 6, Pre-emption Road.

35.2 Between the brick pillars, turn right onto White Springs Lane. *From 1790, White Springs Farm's 1,600 acres was the anomalous home of "Virginia plantation life, modified by climate and the laws of the state affecting the holding of slaves." Later it was owned by a succession of wealthy gentlemen farmers and had prizewinning breeding stock of shorthorns and Guernseys. The present buildings date from 1900 to 1902.*

35.9 At the T-junction, turn left.

36.1 Turn right onto St. Clair Street.

37.0 Soon you'll see the athletic fields of Hobart–William Smith. You will reach your starting point in another mile or so. *For an elegant end to the day, you might visit Belhurst Castle, about 2 miles south of Hobart on NY 14. Formerly a casino, this outstanding 1890 Richardsonian Romanesque mansion has six guest rooms "for the discriminating traveler." Lunch and dinner are served daily in season, and the spacious lawns and lake view are open to all (315-781-0201). More modest accommodations can be found at Virginia Deane's Bed and Breakfast, opposite the Hobart campus at 168 Hamilton Street (315-789-6152).*

Nearby Bed-and-Breakfasts

LaFayette B&B, 107 LaFayette Avenue, Geneva (315-781-0068)

Virginia Deane's B&B, 168 Hamilton Street, Geneva (315-789-6152)

Bicycle Shops

Geneva Bicycle Center, 489 Exchange Street, Geneva (315-789-5922)

Snow Country Bike Shop, Parkway Plaza, NY 5 and US 20, Canandaigua (585-394-1530)

—Updated by Jim Finkle

5

Canandaigua–Vine Valley

- ■ **DISTANCE:** 26 miles; moderate cycling
- ■ **TERRAIN:** Level to rolling terrain with long, gradual hills
- ■ **COUNTY MAPS:** Ontario, Yates

Fine views of lake and vineyards abound in this tour along the east side of 16-mile-long Canandaigua Lake. The first half of the ride parallels the lakeshore, with a convenient lunch or rest stop at the appropriately named Vine Valley. (An optional diversion offers a few more miles of lakeside riding south of the valley.) From Vine Valley the route climbs inland to the village of Rushville, birthplace of the Oregon Trail pioneer Marcus Whitman. A high and little-used ridge road leads back to the city of Canandaigua, affording excellent views of the northern part of the lake and an exhilarating freewheel down a long, gentle hill. There are opportunities for swimming and fishing along the lake's east side and at its north end, where the tour starts and finishes. Those with time to spare can hike nature trails on the campus of the Finger Lakes Community College. Outdoor concerts by the Rochester Philharmonic Orchestra are given on summer weekends at the Finger Lakes Performing Arts Center located on the campus.

The tour begins at the parking area for the Finger Lakes Performing Arts Center. The parking lot can be reached by taking the first or second left turn off NY 364 (East Lake Road) south of Lakeshore Drive.

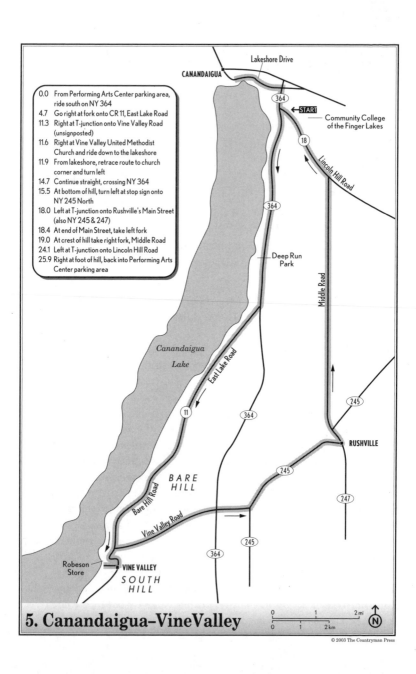

Lakeshore Drive

CANANDAIGUA

364

←START

Community College
of the Finger Lakes

18

Lincoln Hill Road

0.0	From Performing Arts Center parking area, ride south on NY 364
4.7	Go right at fork onto CR 11, East Lake Road
11.3	Right at T-junction onto Vine Valley Road (unsignposted)
11.6	Right at Vine Valley United Methodist Church and ride down to the lakeshore
11.9	From lakeshore, retrace route to church corner and turn left
14.7	Continue straight, crossing NY 364
15.5	At bottom of hill, turn left at stop sign onto NY 245 North
18.0	Left at T-junction onto Rushville's Main Street (also NY 245 & 247)
18.4	At end of Main Street, take left fork
19.0	At crest of hill take right fork, Middle Road
24.1	Left at T-junction onto Lincoln Hill Road
25.9	Right at foot of hill, back into Performing Arts Center parking area

364

Deep Run
Park

Middle Road

Canandaigua
Lake

East Lake Road

11

364

245

RUSHVILLE

BARE
HILL

Bare Hill Road

245

247

Vine Valley Road

Robeson
Store

VINE VALLEY

SOUTH
HILL

245

364

0   1   2 mi
0   1   2 km

N

5. Canandaigua–VineValley

0.0 From the parking area for the Performing Arts Center, ride south on NY 364.

Those wishing to carry food with them will find several supermarkets in town. The most extravagant selection of deli, bakery, gourmet, and natural foods is at local favorite Wegmans (open 24 hours), about a mile east of Main Street on Eastern Boulevard (NY 5 and US 20).

NY 364 can get an uncomfortable amount of traffic on summer weekends, and its shoulder is intermittent; the good news is that you'll be on this road for less than 5 miles. Three miles along NY 364 is Deep Run Park, where facilities include picnic tables, rest rooms, and drinking fountains. The major attraction of Deep Run is its bathing beach; fishing may be possible in spring and fall, or when no swimmers are present.

One-half mile farther on you'll see Thendara Inn and Restaurant, which overlooks the lake. Shortly after 1900 it was built as a retirement home by John Raines, a state senator and U.S. congressman; the 14-room mansion was completed just before his death. Thendara's special feature is its Boathouse, where light meals and drinks are served 11:30 AM–9 PM daily from May to October. Rooms are available in the inn over the restaurant.

4.7 At the fork, go right onto CR 11, East Lake Road. About 2.5 miles down CR 11, a mile-long hill begins that takes you up about 350 feet. Here the road climbs a flank of Bare Hill (elevation 1,540 feet), which, with neighboring South Hill (elevation 1,893 feet), figures prominently in the mythology of the Seneca Indians.

Bare Hill, called Genundawah by the Senecas, was sacred to the tribe. According to legend, the hill was once encircled by an enormous two-headed serpent that devoured the Seneca inhabitants. A young warrior, instructed in a dream to string his bow with the hair of his young sister, finally slew the serpent. In its death throes the serpent tumbled down the hillside, tearing up the vegetation and disgorging the heads of the Senecas it had eaten. Although wooded now, Bare Hill is said to have been free of trees when white men first saw it. The Seneca rite of lighting ceremonial fires yearly on Bare Hill is echoed by lake property owners who, signaled by a flare atop Bare Hill, light a Ring of Fire around Canandaigua Lake on the Saturday evening before Labor Day.

Soon after Bare Hill turns from antagonist to helper, it becomes clear that the name Vine Valley is not fanciful. Vineyards carpet the gentle bowl of the valley floor. Depending on the season, you may see workers tying up vines before the growing season, large green leaves hiding tiny grape clusters, or heavy masses of golden, russet, or purple grapes. On warm autumn days the smell, as well as the sight, is heavenly.

11.3 Turn right at the T-junction onto Vine Valley Road (unsignposted). Caution: Vine Valley Road drops sharply and, in about 100 feet, makes a 180-degree turn.

A state historical marker at this junction notes the 1922 excavation of a Native American burial ground in Vine Valley. It is believed to be a grave site of early Woodland Indians of the Adena culture, thought to have migrated from Ohio, bringing with them an appreciation of finely made stone objects and a tradition of building mound graves. The artifacts of pottery, bone, antler, and stone recovered from the Vine Valley graves are dated between 500 b.c. and a.d. 500.

11.6 At the Vine Valley United Methodist Church (1891), turn right and ride down to the lakeshore.

The Robeson General Store, near the lake, was already a Vine Valley landmark by the turn of the 20th century. It once housed dances, church socials, and long winter chats; in recent years it has reopened as a quaint general store. Adjacent property was purchased by the town, which has installed picnic tables and a swimming beach beside the old building.

In the old days, Vine Valley was an important stop for Canandaigua Lake steamboats bringing goods to the store and picnickers to Willow Grove, a recreation area that is now a trailer park. Holidaymakers could buy a special ticket at the Canandaigua City Pier good for a day's outing at Willow Grove and return to Canandaigua on a moonlight cruise. In addition to summer revelers, the steamers once carried grapes, apples, and other produce to Canandaigua and thence to other cities. Travel by water became so much easier than by land that the steamers put the Canandaigua-to-Naples stagecoach out of business. In the 20th century, improved roads and automobiles made land travel more efficient, and most of the steamers disappeared by World War I.

11.9 From the lakeshore, retrace your route to the church corner and turn left. Follow the road around the 180-degree turn, up the steep grade, keeping to the right. Do not turn left onto the road that brought you to Vine Valley. As you climb, Bare Hill is to your left, South Hill to your right.

For a few more miles of quiet lakeside riding, one can add the following diversion: Turn right, instead of left, at the Vine Valley church. Follow this road as it bends

A reproduction of the steamboats that used to ply the waters of the Finger Lakes

right, down to the lake, and then left. This road dead ends, so traffic is light. A little more than 2 miles from Vine Valley is Whiskey Point, where a still once operated. A whiskey scow sank near the Point and is presumably there yet. One can ride for about 3 miles before it is necessary to turn around and return to Vine Valley. Although there is no official public access, cyclists interested in fishing can ask permission of lakeshore residents.

14.7 Continue straight, crossing NY 364.
A well-preserved one-room brick school dated 1874 is located on the northwest corner of this intersection, known locally as Overacker Corners. It was in use until 1937.

15.5 At the bottom of the hill, turn left at the stop sign onto NY 245 North.
Along this stretch you'll pass the Marcus Whitman public school, named in honor of Rushville's most famous son.

18.0 Turn left at the T-junction onto Rushville's Main Street, which is also NY 245 and 247.
The village was originally called Federal Hollow; the name was changed during the

War of 1812 when the Federalist Party opposed the locally popular war. The new name honored Dr. Benjamin Rush, a signer of the Declaration of Independence and a Democrat.

On the left, 1 block after turning onto Main Street, you'll see a marker commemorating the birthplace of Dr. Marcus Whitman, born on September 4, 1802. Whitman traveled the Oregon Trail twice, the second time with his wife, Narcissa Prentiss, one of the first two white women to cross the Rockies. More of Whitman's story is recounted in Tour 19.

18.4 At the end of Main Street, take the left fork, following a straight course as NY 245 and 247 bear right. The uphill lasts about 0.75 mile.

19.0 At the crest of the hill, take the right fork, Middle Road.

24.1 Turn left at the T-junction onto Lincoln Hill Road.
Soon you will have good views to the foot of Canandaigua Lake, including Squaw Island, one of two islands in the Finger Lakes and the smallest state park in New York. Legend has it that Seneca women and children were hidden on the island from General Sullivan's expedition of 1779.

25.9 Turn right at the foot of the hill back into the Performing Arts Center parking area, where the tour began.
The Finger Lakes Performing Arts Center is the summer home of the Rochester Philharmonic Orchestra, which performs on summer weekends. Numerous popular music events are scheduled during June, July, and August. The concert shell, which seats 2,600 under the roof, is located at the foot of a hill that overlooks the lake. Thousands more come to picnic on the lawn, where they can enjoy the concerts and watch the sun set over the lake. Program information can be obtained by calling the ticket office at 716-394-7190.

Finger Lakes Community College also has two marked nature trails, tennis courts, and an air-conditioned cafeteria and library. Cafeteria summer hours are 7:30 AM–2 PM weekdays and 5–8:30 PM Monday through Thursday.

At the parking area's northwest entrance is the Lincoln Hill Inn, serving Continental specialties to concertgoers and other guests.

Swimming and picnicking are available at newly renovated Kershaw Park, located on Lakeshore Drive at the north end of the lake. Here and farther along to the west on Lakeshore Drive a variety of snack bars and restaurants can be found, including Steamboat Landing on the lakefront at the east end of Kershaw Park. At the west end of the park is the City Pier, which dates from 1845, when $1,000 was spent on its construction. Makeshift boathouses lined the west side of the pier until a 1903 beautification scheme had them removed to the lateral arms, where they remain—picturesque, charming, or dilapidated, depending on your viewpoint.

Short launch tours of the lake operate from the Inn on the Lake (adjacent to the City Pier). For schedules and fares call Captain Gray's Boat Tours, 716-394-5270. The Inn on the Lake offers comfortable rooms and lakeside dining, indoors or on the patio. Boat rentals or fishing charters can be arranged at the base of the pier at Seager Marine, 716-394-1372. Behind Seager's on Lakeshore Drive, you'll find sailboard rentals. Those seeking more immobile pursuits can feed the ducks or browse at the Waterfront Art Festival, held at the City Pier annually on the first weekend in August.

There are numerous bed-and-breakfasts and a variety of lodging establishments in the area. A listing can be found at the Canandaigua Chamber of Commerce web site, www.canandaigua.com.

Nearby Bed-and-Breakfasts

Acorn Inn, 4508 Route 64 S, Canandaigua (1-888-245-4134)

1885 Sutherland House B&B Inn, 3179 NY 21 South, Canandaigua (1-800-396-0375)

Habersham Country Inn, 6124 NY 5 and US 20, Canandaigua (1-866-724-2601)

Inn on the Lake, 770 South Main Street, Canandaigua (585-394-7800; 1-800-228-2801)

Morgan Samuels Inn, 2920 Smith Road, Canandaigua (585-394-9232)

Oliver Phelps Country Inn, 252 North Main Street, Canandaigua (585-396-1650)

Bicycle Shops

Geneva Bicycle Center, 489 Exchange Street, Geneva (315-789-5922)

Park Avenue Bike Shop, Parkway Plaza, NY 5 and US 20, Canandaigua (585-398-2300)

—Updated by Tom Wood

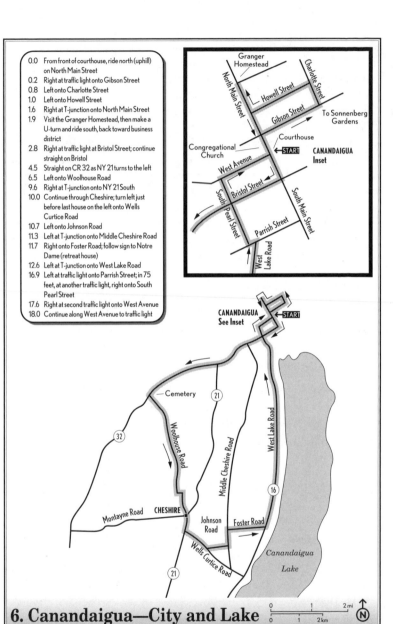

0.0 From front of courthouse, ride north (uphill) on North Main Street
0.2 Right at traffic light onto Gibson Street
0.8 Left onto Charlotte Street
1.0 Left onto Howell Street
1.6 Right at T-junction onto North Main Street
1.9 Visit the Granger Homestead, then make a U-turn and ride south, back toward business district
2.8 Right at traffic light at Bristol Street; continue straight on Bristol
4.5 Straight on CR 32 as NY 21 turns to the left
6.5 Left onto Woolhouse Road
9.6 Right at T-junction onto NY 21 South
10.0 Continue through Cheshire; turn left just before last house on the left onto Wells Curtice Road
10.7 Left onto Johnson Road
11.3 Left at T-junction onto Middle Cheshire Road
11.7 Right onto Foster Road; follow sign to Notre Dame (retreat house)
12.6 Left at T-junction onto West Lake Road
16.9 Left at traffic light onto Parrish Street; in 75 feet, at another traffic light, right onto South Pearl Street
17.6 Right at second traffic light onto West Avenue
18.0 Continue along West Avenue to traffic light

CANANDAIGUA Inset

Granger Homestead
North Main Street
Charlotte Street
Howell Street
Gibson Street
To Sonnenberg Gardens
Congregational Church
Courthouse
←START
West Avenue
Bristol Street
South Pearl Street
South Main Street
Parrish Street
West Lake Road

CANANDAIGUA See Inset
←START

Cemetery
(21)
West Lake Road
(32)
Woolhouse Road
Middle Cheshire Road
(16)
Montayne Road
CHESHIRE
Johnson Road
Foster Road
Wells Curtice Road
(21)
Canandaigua Lake

6. Canandaigua—City and Lake

0   1   2 mi
0   1   2 km
N

Canandaigua—City and Lake

- **DISTANCE:** 18 miles; easy to moderate cycling
- **TERRAIN:** Flat terrain with some low hills
- **COUNTY MAP:** Ontario

In 1832 Englishwoman Frances Trollope wrote of Canandaigua: "It is as pretty a village as ever man contrived to build. Every house is surrounded by an ample garden . . . and half buried in roses." Earlier, in 1804, Robert Munro reported that some of Canandaigua's houses were "elegant," and that "many of its inhabitants are wealthy in circumstances." Along the city's wide and shaded streets, many fine houses in a great variety of architectural styles are still seen, including the much visited Sonnenberg Gardens and Mansion. But city quickly gives way to farm and orchard. This route also visits the quiet village of Cheshire and includes several miles of cool riding along the shore of Canandaigua Lake, passing a public swimming beach. For combining historic and architectural interest with country scenery and pleasant riding, it is a tour hard to equal.

You may wish to start your tour with a visit to the flagship store of the Wegmans supermarket chain, located on NY 5 and US 20. The Wegmans company was cited in the *Wall Street Journal* as the leading grocer in the country. You can buy provisions for your ride here or have a meal on the Marketplace Café patio.

The ride begins in the city of Canandaigua in front of the county courthouse on North Main Street. The golden-domed courthouse is visible for miles around.

0.0 From the front of the courthouse, ride north (uphill) on North Main Street.

The present Ontario County Court House dates from 1857 to 1858. Its most famous trial occurred in 1873 when Susan B. Anthony was found guilty of voting and fined $100. Anthony actually voted in Rochester, where her house is now maintained as a museum, but a change of venue brought the case to Canandaigua. In a move of doubtful legality, the judge dismissed the jury and directed a guilty verdict, but the fine was never paid, nor was any other punishment exacted. On the front lawn of the courthouse is the "council rock," site of the signing of the Pickering Treaty on November 11, 1794, between the U.S. Government and the Iroquois Nation.

Just up the street, at 55 North Main, is a 1913 Georgian Revival building housing the Ontario County Historical Society. In addition to its changing exhibits, the society provides several brochures with detailed architectural tours of the city, plus other publications on local history. The building is open Tuesday through Saturday 10 AM–5 PM (Wednesday until 9 PM). Admission is $2 for the museum, $5 for the research library.

0.2 Turn right at the traffic light onto Gibson Street.

Number 29, the first of three impressive Federal-style houses on Gibson Street, was once the home of Myron Holley Clark (1806–92), the only Temperance governor of New York and the father of Mary Clark Thompson, benefactress of the city and creator of Sonnenberg Gardens.

0.8 Turn left onto Charlotte Street. This corner also has a sign to the VA Medical Center and Sonnenberg Gardens.

Charlotte Street is shaded by plane trees planted by one of Sonnenberg's landscape architects, John Handrahan, in 1903. Mary Clark married Frederick Ferris Thompson, a founder of the First National Bank of New York, in 1857. By 1887 they had completed Sonnenberg as their summer home; the elaborate gardens were added by the widowed Mrs. Thompson from 1902 to 1916. The mansion shows various architectural influences—unified by a style perhaps best called Pre-Income Tax Opulent. Refurbished and refurnished, the house is a fascinating Victorian testament to how the other 1 percent lived. On Sonnenberg's 50 acres the Italian, Rose, Japanese, Colonial, and Rock Gardens have been restored to their former glory. The Italian Garden is filled with tulips in May, and continues with begonias and other annuals through the summer; the roses peak in late June. Sonnenberg Gardens and Mansion are open daily 9:30 AM–5:30 PM Mother's

Outdoor musical and theater performances attract crowds to Canandaigua's Sonnenberg Gardens.

Day through mid-October, with special musical and theatrical performances scheduled occasionally. Admission is $8.50 for adults and $3.50 for those under 16. Sonnenberg's Peach House Restaurant, in a former greenhouse, with outdoor tables, serves light lunches and elaborate desserts 11:30 AM–3:30 PM May through September.

1.0 Turn left onto Howell Street. On your right at this corner are the massive wrought-iron gates of the entrance to Sonnenberg.
Howell Street is one of the most pleasant residential streets in the city. Altogether its houses provide a convenient compendium of popular 19th-century styles: Federal, Greek Revival, Italianate, Second Empire, Eastlake, Tudor, Queen Anne.

1.6 Turn right at the T-junction onto North Main Street.

1.9 The Granger Homestead, to your right, is as far up Main Street as this tour extends. When you have seen or visited the Homestead, make a U-turn and ride south, downhill, back toward the business district.
The Granger Homestead at 295 North Main Street was built about 1816 for

Gideon Granger, postmaster general under Presidents Jefferson and Madison. This predominantly Federal-style building was also home to Gideon's son, Francis, another postmaster general, and later it housed a girls school. The elegant interior is described on guided tours given Tuesday through Sunday 1–5 PM, with the last tour leaving at 4 PM. Admission is $5 for adults and $1 for students. Children under six are free.

The Homestead's carriage house displays the second largest collection of horse-drawn vehicles in New York. It includes the carriage of Jemima Wilkinson, one of the odd religious figures of the region, who settled in 1791 with her followers near Keuka Lake. This self-styled prophetess called herself the Publick Universal Friend, and the initials UF can still be barely discerned on the rear and door of her carriage.

A short distance down Main Street from the Granger Homestead is the Elm Manor Nursing Home at number 210. The front portion of the complex was built in 1797 for Peter B. Porter, but it was home to several men of note—a U.S. senator and two presidential cabinet secretaries. Peter Porter was secretary of war under John Q. Adams; he was also an influential early backer of the Erie Canal and later contributed greatly to the development of the Buffalo area. Senator Elbridge G. Lapham is best remembered for leading Senate ratification of the Geneva Convention in 1882. John Spencer had a successful legal and political career (holding two cabinet posts), but he is chiefly remembered for being the unfortunate father of a more unfortunate son, Philip Spencer. Philip was born here, walked across the street to school, and spent several desultory years at Hobart College in Geneva. While his father was secretary of war, Philip joined the Navy, was involved in strange goings-on aboard ship, and was precipitously hanged at sea on December 1, 1842, on the charge of attempted mutiny. The incident produced a sensation in its time and provided Herman Melville with the storyline for his novella Billy Budd.

The Congregational church at 58 North Main Street is perhaps the most interesting public building in the city. Built in 1812, its harmonious rectangular form is enlivened by an arched entranceway. The fine interior features box pews with the original doors and hinges. Though it has been known as the Old Brick, it seems that the church has always been painted, often necessary to protect weak, locally pressed brick from weathering. The father of social critic Max Eastman was pastor here in the late 19th century, and Max was born at the parsonage (built c. 1830) at 116 East Gibson Street, behind the small, parklike square.

On the right, at the corner of West Avenue, is the city hall building. It was built *in 1824 and served as the courthouse until the present one was constructed.*

2.8 When you have passed through most of the business district, you'll come to a traffic light at Bristol Street, where you make a right turn. Continue straight on Bristol out of town.

Near the edge of town, just before Bristol Street goes briefly downhill, you may notice a bronze plaque on a stone gatepost to the left. It notes that the Sullivan-Clinton campaign to destroy the Iroquois, allied with the British, passed here on September 11 and 18, 1779. The gateposts lead to Brigham Hall, built in 1855 as a private hospital for the insane. Later used as a nursing home and now converted into apartments, much of the hospital's careful landscaping can still be seen. From Canandaigua, Sullivan's army marched over the hills to Honeoye, and two days later it reached the Genesee River. For the next 3 or so miles our route roughly follows the army's line of march.

4.5 Go straight on CR 32 as NY 21 turns to the left.

6.5 Turn left onto Woolhouse Road.
At this corner is a cemetery with graves dating from the beginning of European settlement in the area.

If you want to extend the tour by about 4 miles to include some challenging hill climbing, do not turn left on Woolhouse Road. Instead, continue straight on CR 32 another 4 miles, turning left there onto Montayne Road. Following this road will take you over high hills and into the village of Cheshire.

9.6 Turn right at the T-junction onto NY 21 South.
To the right is a former public school that now houses The Company Store, which has an excellent selection of food, including freshly prepared sandwiches and pastries. It's open in summer daily 6:30 AM–10 PM. There are picnic tables by the playing field behind the school, or you can eat at tables in one of the old schoolrooms.

10.0 Continue through the village of Cheshire and turn left just before the last house on the left onto Wells Curtice Road.

10.7 Turn left onto Johnson Road.
Along Johnson Road killdeer are often seen and heard. When they run before taking flight, their white wing patches show clearly. Their piping whistle is often the loudest sound heard here.

11.3 Turn left at the T-junction onto Middle Cheshire Road.

11.7 Turn right onto Foster Road, also following the sign to Notre Dame (retreat house).

The lower half of Foster Road passes between abandoned orchards—apple, pear, peach, cherry. In blossom time, about mid-May, it combines the pleasures of an Impressionist painting and a perfume distillery.

Care is needed as Foster Road comes to an end; the final 100 or so feet are very steep, and the intersection is usually slippery with loose sand and gravel.

12.6 Turn left at the T-junction onto West Lake Road.

Along West Lake Road you might note a couple of cobblestone houses. This is south of the area where building with cobblestones was common in the second third of the 19th century, and it is likely that the cobbles were carted here from a spot near the Lake Ontario shore.

Two and a half miles farther, where Butler Road enters from the left, is a small public swimming area. The one-room school across the road had classes until the 1960s and is now used for a youth summer recreation program.

A half mile north of Butler Road is the Canandaigua Yacht Club. Races are scheduled for most Sunday mornings. If you're interested in watching these often-colorful events, or in perhaps offering to crew, schedule details can be had by calling 585-396-9200 in Canandaigua or 585-924-3100 in Rochester.

16.9 Turn left at the traffic light onto Parrish Street, and in 75 feet, at another traffic light, turn right onto South Pearl Street.

17.6 Turn right at the second traffic light onto West Avenue.

On your right, you'll pass Canandaigua's Pioneer Cemetery. Among the oldest graves is that of Oliver Phelps, of the famous Phelps-Gorham Purchase, which opened western New York to settlement.

18.0 Continuing along West Avenue to the traffic light will bring you to Main Street and the Ontario County Court House.

This would be a great time to enjoy a snack at the Catskill Bagel & Deli Company, just down the road at 103 South Main Street. Excellent homemade bagels and muffins can be enjoyed inside or on the patio.

Nearby Bed-and-Breakfasts

Clawson's B&B, 3615 Lincoln Hill Road, Canandaigua (585-396-1947)

Habersham Country Inn, 6124 NY 5 and US 20, Canandaigua (585-394-1510)

Inn on the Lake, 770 South Main Street, Canandaigua (585-394-7800; 1-800-228-2801)

J.P. Morgan House, 2920 Smith Road, Canandaigua (585-394-9232)

Oliver Phelps Country Inn, 252 North Main Street, Canandaigua (585-396-1650)

Sutherland House B&B Inn, 3179 NY 21 South, Canandaigua (1-800-396-0375)

Bicycle Shops

Snow Country Bike Shop, Parkway Plaza, NY 5 and US 20, Canandaigua (585-394-1530)

—Updated by Robbie Finkle

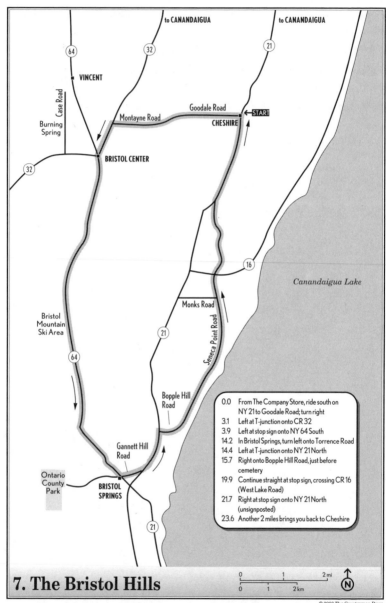

to CANANDAIGUA   to CANANDAIGUA

64

32

21

VINCENT

Case Road

Goodale Road

Burning
Spring

Montayne Road ◄START

CHESHIRE

BRISTOL CENTER

32

16

Canandaigua Lake

Monks Road

Bristol
Mountain
Ski Area

21

Seneca Point Road

64

Bopple Hill
Road

Gannett Hill
Road

Ontario
County
Park

BRISTOL
SPRINGS

21

0.0 From The Company Store, ride south on
   NY 21 to Goodale Road; turn right
3.1 Left at T-junction onto CR 32
3.9 Left at stop sign onto NY 64 South
14.2 In Bristol Springs, turn left onto Torrence Road
14.4 Left at T-junction onto NY 21 North
15.7 Right onto Bopple Hill Road, just before
   cemetery
19.9 Continue straight at stop sign, crossing CR 16
   (West Lake Road)
21.7 Right at stop sign onto NY 21 North
   (unsignposted)
23.6 Another 2 miles brings you back to Cheshire

7. The Bristol Hills

0   1   2 mi

0 1 2 km

N

The Bristol Hills

- **DISTANCE:** 24 miles; moderate to strenuous cycling
- **TERRAIN:** Rolling to hilly terrain with some level sections
- **COUNTY MAP:** Ontario

The Bristol Hills form the highest and some of the most rugged, attractive scenery in the Finger Lakes. Their once sparse farm population has broadened recently to include independent crafts-people and antiques dealers who have found niches in the steep-sided valleys and wooded hilltops. This tour links quiet villages via roads that give the cyclist strenuous climbs rewarded by distant views and swift descents. It passes Bristol Mountain, a downhill ski center.

Bristol Mountain's 1,200-foot vertical rise is the tallest of any ski area between the Adirondack/Catskill region and the Rocky Mountains. From mid-September until the end of October, Bristol also offers chairlift rides to view the spectacular fall colors.

Leaving a road high above Canandaigua Lake, you drop rapidly to enjoy a couple of miles of shore riding along the lake's most affluent "cottage" area. Quiet back roads are used except for a few miles in the Bristol Valley and a short distance on NY 21.

The tour starts in the village of Cheshire at The Company Store—housed in a converted school building—on the west side of NY 21. We suggest leaving your car at the little park on Goodale Road.

0.0 From the front of The Company Store, ride south on NY 21 for 50 yards until you come to Goodale Road. Turn right at this junction.

The Company Store provides the makings of a fine picnic, including cold drinks, hot coffee, and freshly made sandwiches. Company Store summer hours are 6:30 AM–10 PM daily. You'll find picnic tables behind the store near the playing field, and more tables in the town park on Goodale Road. If you prefer, you can eat indoors in a former schoolroom, or shop for antiques upstairs.

Cheshire straddles a state highway, but the pace of the village is more aptly characterized by the dogs that saunter unhurriedly along its main street. First called Klipknocket, it seems appropriate that the village was afterward known as Idle Corners, the final name change coming at the behest of immigrants from Cheshire in Connecticut.

Goodale Road climbs about 400 feet in the first mile after leaving Cheshire, reaching an elevation of 1,420 feet. You'll find beautiful views of the Bristol Hills from here. After the crest is passed, Goodale Road is called Montayne Road; this is because each road dead-ended until recently, when the two were linked by the road over the hills.

3.1 At the T-junction, turn left onto CR 32.
In a few yards you'll be looking into the Bristol Valley and facing a nearly mile-long downhill. Don't let generally good paving lull you into freewheeling too fast. Stop and explore the old cemetery on your right, about halfway down the hill.

3.9 At the stop sign at the bottom of the hill, turn left onto NY 64 South.
Food supplies can be obtained here at the Clement's Country Store or Bristol Trading Post.

The French explorer La Salle is said to have visited Bristol Valley in 1669 while searching for the Mississippi's source. It is said that local Native Americans took La Salle, perhaps the first white man they had seen, to their miraculous Burning Spring. To visit the site of the Burning Spring, go straight across NY 64 at the bottom of the long hill, continuing west on CR 32. In 0.7 mile turn right onto the unpaved Case Road. A half mile farther you'll see a marker for the Burning Spring just beyond a small stream. When Capt. Basil Hall, a British traveler, did what you are doing in 1827, he noted that "on reaching the spot, we discovered a spring to be sure, but could see no flames. . . . I was beginning to feel that awkward sort of distrust which accompanies the suspicion of being quizzed, and sent on a fool's errand; when behold! the air caught fire, and in a few minutes, we had a row of natural gas lights blazing in a style worthy of Pall-Mall. . . ." It is believed that natural gas escapes beneath water and bubbles to the surface, where it can be ignited. We've never seen it done, but if you want to try you should ask permission at the house, as the stream is on private property.

From the Burning Spring, retrace your route to the intersection with NY 64, and there turn south. In all, this diversion adds 2.8 miles to the tour.

The Bristol Valley is a typical glacial valley, with a flat bottom and steep, wooded sides. A surprising amount of what appears to be useful, easily worked bottomland is unfarmed scrub and brush. Some blame this on overgrazing by sheep in the 19th century. Two miles north of the village of Bristol Center was another called Muttonville; between 1830 and 1850 it had the nation's largest sheep slaughter-house, and the Bristol Valley was temporary home to some fifty thousand sheep. Today Muttonville has been renamed Vincent after a pioneer physician, and almost no sheep are seen.

About halfway down the valley you pass a small pub called Lock's Stock and Barrell, where old bicycles, among other unusual items, hang from the ceiling. A mile or so south is the Bristol Mountain Ski and Snowboard Center.

14.2 In the hamlet of Bristol Springs, turn left onto Torrence Road. Provisions can be obtained here at Hovey House Café and Bakery, which also serves breakfast and lunch. Look around the tiny area of Bristol Springs for antiques shops, a unique clothing store, and some eateries. The Arbor Hill Grapery offers wine tasting and cheese.

If you turn right instead of left at this corner, you can visit Ontario County Park atop 2,256-foot-high Gannett Hill, the highest elevation in the Finger Lakes and the site of the University of Rochester's Mees Observatory. It's a hard climb of about a mile and a half to reach the park, but if you're interested in camping, the setting and facilities are ideal. The park also has picnic tables and shelters, rest rooms, and hiking trails. Orange tree blazes mark the Bristol Hill spur of the Finger Lakes Trail, which snakes east–west for 100 miles or so across the southern Finger Lakes. The most striking views are in the vicinity of the Jump-off, to which there are many signs. From there you look down into West Hollow, a glacial valley narrower and steeper than the one through which you have just ridden. Cars far below look like toys, and small farmsteads quilt the valley in shades of green.

Gannett Hill takes its name from the first family to settle the area. Frank Gannett was born on a hill farm here in 1876; he went on to found what is today America's largest newspaper chain.

14.4 Turn left at the T-junction onto NY 21 North. NY 21 gets some fast traffic; intermittently it has a ridable shoulder.

CHIP SAHLER

A Canandaigua Lake vista as seen from Bopple Hill

15.7 Just before reaching a small cemetery, turn right onto Bopple Hill Road. *Bopple Hill is very steep, but fortunately the road is paved. Old-timers tell of wagons loaded with grapes being skidded down Bopple Hill with their wheels locked— otherwise the wagons would have overrun the horses.*

With wet or questionable brakes it would be safest to walk down Bopple Hill, or to follow the alternative route suggested below. If you decide to ride down the hill, you should pull both brake levers with all your strength before starting down. If a cable is going to snap—and in time all cables do—you'll be safer if it breaks while you have both feet on the ground.

If you prefer not to ride down Bopple Hill, simply continue north on NY 21 for about 3 miles and turn right onto Monks Road. In about a mile, Monks Road ends at Seneca Point Road, where you should turn left to rejoin the tour route shortly before it crosses CR 16.

Directly across the lake from Bopple Hill Road is Vine Valley, with Bare Hill to the north and South Hill, or The Whaleback, to the south. A Seneca Indian legend about Bare Hill is recounted in Tour 5.

At lake level you'll find that Bopple Hill Road is now called Seneca Point Road.

A mile and a half farther along, just before a long uphill, is Seneca Point, probably the most fashionable address on the lake. The summer colony here once included such well-known New Yorkers as builder Robert Moses, New York World *reporter Herbert Bayard Swope, and Thomas Fogarty, illustrator for* Cosmopolitan *and* The Saturday Evening Post*. Humphrey Bogart spent summers at Seneca Point as a child in his parents' cottage. Even Franklin Delano Roosevelt visited friends here in the 1920s.*

After Seneca Point, the road climbs steeply and gradually for almost 2 miles. At the top of the hill you will find the Bristol Lodge and golf course on your left. The lodge offers excellent casual dining with an incredible view. A little farther on your right is the South Bristol Cultural Center, which often exhibits works of local artists.

19.9 Continue straight at the stop sign, crossing CR 16 (also known as West Lake Road).

21.7 Turn right at the stop sign onto NY 21 North (unsignposted).

23.6 You are now back in Cheshire.

Nearby Bed-and-Breakfasts

Acorn Inn, 4508 NY 64 South, Bristol Center, Canandaigua (585-229-2834, 1-888-245-4134; www.acorninnbb.com)

The Filigree Inn, 5406 NY 64, Bristol (585-229-5460)

Bicycle Shops

Snow Country Bike Shop, Parkway Plaza, NY 5 and US 20, Canandaigua (585-394-1530)

—Updated by Jon Maltese

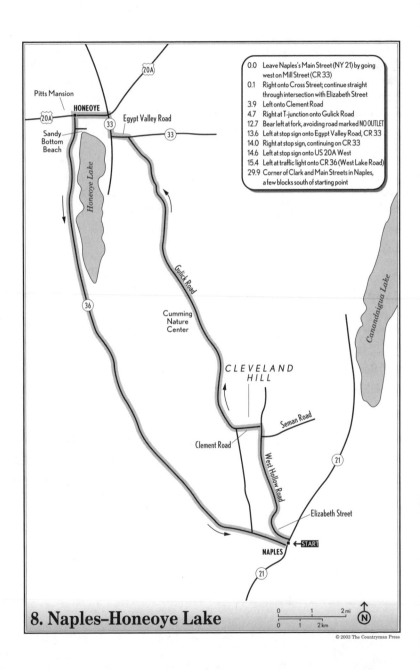

0.0	Leave Naples's Main Street (NY 21) by going west on Mill Street (CR 33)
0.1	Right onto Cross Street; continue straight through intersection with Elizabeth Street
3.9	Left onto Clement Road
4.7	Right at T-junction onto Gulick Road
12.7	Bear left at fork, avoiding road marked NO OUTLET
13.6	Left at stop sign onto Egypt Valley Road, CR 33
14.0	Right at stop sign, continuing on CR 33
14.6	Left at stop sign onto US 20A West
15.4	Left at traffic light onto CR 36 (West Lake Road)
29.9	Corner of Clark and Main Streets in Naples, a few blocks south of starting point

Pitts Mansion

HONEOYE

Egypt Valley Road

Sandy Bottom Beach

Honeoye Lake

Gulick Road

Cumming Nature Center

CLEVELAND HILL

Seman Road

Clement Road

West Hollow Road

Canandaigua Lake

Elizabeth Street

START

NAPLES

8. Naples–Honeoye Lake

0   1   2 mi
0   1   2 km

N

© 2003 The Countryman Press

Naples–Honeoye Lake

- **DISTANCE:** 30 miles; moderate cycling
- **TERRAIN:** Low rolling hills, with one steep section
- **COUNTY MAP:** Ontario

Even though this tour goes for miles through wooded and farmed countryside and takes in only two small villages, it offers something for everyone, from the artist and theatergoer to the oenophile and gourmet. Except for a few miles bordering Honeoye Lake, most of the roads get very little traffic, although one should be alert on fine weekends in September and October when fall foliage lures tourists—many also to be enticed by autumn entrepreneurs selling Grandma's bustle, pictures of Great-Grandpa in his Civil War uniform, or genuine leaky wine casks. Naples also attracts visitors to view its vineyard-clad hills, tour the winery, hike trails to scenic overlooks, and fish its trout streams. Small galleries display the work of artists and craftspeople from the village and surrounding hills.

Honeoye, smaller than Naples and more influenced by plastics technology, would have disappeared altogether had the city of Rochester had its way in the 1930s and flooded the place for an enlarged reservoir. A visit to Sandy Bottom swimming beach near the village provides a view down the length of Honeoye Lake that will make you glad it's still as the glaciers left it. There are four nature reserves on or near this tour; most have picnic tables, but you should pack your own meals as there are few restaurants or stores outside the two towns.

The tour starts in Naples, located at the south end of Canandaigua Lake on NY 21.

0.0 Leave Naples's Main Street (NY 21) by going west on Mill Street (CR 33) just north of the main block of stores.

Originally called Nunda Wa O—"The Place Between the Hills"—by Native Americans, Naples village is at the confluence of several glacial valleys. Grapes cover 1,200 acres in and around Naples, with 80 percent of them used in wine-making. Swiss-born John Jacob Widmer planted his first vineyard in 1883. It is located just west of the Widmer Winery Visitors' Chalet, and it still bears fruit. Winery tours are offered from June 1 to October 31, 10 AM–4 PM Monday–Saturday and 11:30 AM–4:30 PM Sunday. The Widmer tour is among the most detailed offered by any winery; it is followed by a sit-down wine tasting. Call 1-800-836-LAKE (5253) for information and a free brochure.

Across the street is the 1794 Tellier House. A little to the south, behind the modernistic Catholic church, on Tobey Street, are displays of the Living Wall Garden, designed to grow flowers and vegetables using vertical rather than horizontal space. Economizing on land, water, and fertilizer, these gardens appeal to apartment dwellers and Middle East agricultural officials.

Fishing is popular along Naples Creek, said to be one of the most productive trout streams in the country. More than six thousand people line the creek elbow-to-elbow on April 1, when the Trout Derby opens the season. Public fishing is also permitted at the bridge over Grimes Creek, at the end of Vine Street. It was in Grimes Glen that Archeosigillaria primerium, known as the Naples Tree, was discovered in 1882. The 33-foot-high fossil, now in the State Museum in Albany, provided the first evidence that trees as well as ferns grew in the Devonian period.

Bordering Naples on the east is the High Tor Wildlife Management Area, with nearly 6,000 acres for hunting, fishing, and hiking. High points overlook Canandaigua Lake and valleys south of it. There is easy access to High Tor, and well-cleared trails throughout.

Naples restaurants include The Vineyard at the north end of town, the Naples Hotel in the center, and the Redwood at the southern extreme. There are restaurants in Honeoye as well, and each village has a supermarket.

0.1 Turn right onto Cross Street soon after passing the old mill. In 100 yards, continue straight through the intersection with Elizabeth Street and begin the 700-foot climb out of town. Once out of town, Cross Street becomes West Hollow Road.

Bucolic vineyards in Naples, New York

The uphill from Naples lasts for 1.5 miles and is a rugged way to begin a ride. However, this is the only stiff climb on the tour. Making your way slowly uphill, you may see kingbirds perched on utility lines. This robin-size flycatcher is the only bird around with a white bar across the end of its tail.

When you've finished climbing, look back south toward Naples. You'll see a series of flat-topped hills all reaching about the same height. Geologists cite this as evidence that the region was once quite level, a peneplain later eroded by streams, then carved by glaciers, and now being downcut by streams again.

The first road entering from the right after the climb is Seman Road. About 1.5 miles up Seman you'll find the West Hill Nature Preserve, owned by The Nature Conservancy. On these 300-plus acres, nature is being permitted to make the decisions on land once plowed and cleared by man.

3.9 Turn left onto Clement Road. Here you will also be following signs to Camp Warren Cutler and the Nature Center.

The hill on your right is Cleveland Hill. A sign (perhaps hidden by weeds in summer) beside a dirt track locates the Bristol Hills Branch of the Finger Lakes Trail.

There are good views from 2,000-foot-high Cleveland Hill. To the south the trail passes through Naples, then down Tannery Creek Gorge to High Tor. Maps of the Finger Lakes Trail can be obtained from FLTC, Inc., Box 18048, Twelve Corners Branch, Rochester 14618, or at the Corner Bookstore, on the corner of Main and Race Streets.

4.7 At the T-junction, turn right onto Gulick Road, again following the Nature Center sign. (Sections of Gulick Road are patched and rough.)
About 1 mile down Gulick Road, you'll pass Camp Warren Cutler, a 1,000-acre reservation owned by the Rochester Boy Scouts of America that is devoted to camping and scouting instruction. It is open to visitors year-round.

Two and a half miles farther on you'll reach the entrance to the Cumming Nature Center, whose 819 acres are maintained by the Rochester Museum and Science Center (RMSC). A new Visitors' Building has interpretive exhibits and a gift shop, plus a small cafeteria and rest rooms. Picnic tables are nearby. In addition to several thematic nature trails, Cumming features a farmstead that re-creates the pioneer period of the 1790s, complete with a very popular team of oxen. The center is open weekends only 9 AM–5 PM, January through November 9. Admission is free for RMSC Members; a $3 donation is suggested for nonmembers. Call 585-374-6160 for information about special programs, and for additional information and directions log on to www.rmsc.org.

12.7 Bear left at the fork, avoiding the road marked NO OUTLET.

13.6 At the stop sign, turn left onto Egypt Valley Road, CR 33.

14.0 Turn right at the stop sign, continuing on CR 33.

14.6 Turn left at the stop sign onto US 20A West.
Honeoye is on the route taken by the 1779 Sullivan expedition, which sought to eliminate Native Americans from the region. The Sullivan Monument on the library lawn commemorates the erection of Fort Cummings here. The army sped its march toward the Genesee by leaving at the fort the "sick, lame, and lazy," both equine and human.

The village of Honeoye, originally named Pittstown after its first settler, later took the more mellifluous name of its lake. The Native American word honeoye means "a finger lying."

There are several restaurants and diners in the area, plus a grocery store. Honeoye Commons on Main Street has a restaurant, grocery, gift shop, and phar-

macy. A lovely new gazebo across Main Street is the site of weekly outdoor concerts in the summer.

15.4 Turn left at the traffic light onto CR 36 (West Lake Road).
For a short diversion, continue straight up the hill at this light for about 200 yards, where you'll see a historical marker identifying the Pitts Mansion, built in 1821 by Gideon Pitts, son of the area's first settler. Family sentiments supported abolition, and the house was a station on the Underground Railroad. Gideon's daughter, Helen, caused something of a stir in local and Washington society when she married the escaped slave and abolitionist Frederick Douglass. Both are buried in Rochester's Mount Hope Cemetery. From the Pitts house, return down the hill and turn right at the traffic light.

A half mile down CR 36 (West Lake Road) you'll reach Sandy Bottom Road, which leads to a fine swimming beach. There is a picnic pavilion, and a lifeguard is on duty noon–7 PM (beginning the July 4th weekend and ending about Labor Day).

As you ride south toward the head of Honeoye Lake (recall that all the Finger Lakes drain north), the hills on either side of you heighten, but thanks to the cutting power of the glaciers you will do little climbing. At the head of the lake there is a good view of the wetlands characteristic of the Finger Lakes inlets. Sullivan's men often complained of slogging through miles of "horrid thick Mirey Swamp which render'd our proceeding . . . difficult." South of the lake head the road undulates and weaves pleasantly between hillside vineyards.

29.9 Following a swoop downhill you should be at the corner of Clark and Main Streets in Naples, a few blocks south of your starting point.

Nearby Bed-and-Breakfasts

Acorn Inn, 4508 NY 64 South, Bristol Center, Canandaigua (585-229-2834, 1-888-245-4134; www.acorninnbb.com)

The Filigree Inn, 5406 NY 64, Bristol (585-229-5460)

The Grapevine Inn, 182 Main Street, Naples (585-374-9298)

The Greenwoods, 8136 Quayle Road, Honeoye (585-229-2111)

Maxfield Inn B&B, 105 North Main Street, Naples (585-374-2510)

The Naples Inn, 111 Main Street, Naples (585-374-5630)

The Vagabond Inn, 3300 Slitor Road, Naples (585-554-6271)

Restaurants

Bob & Ruth's Vineyard Restaurant, 204 North Main Street, Naples (585-374-5122)

Bicycle Shops

Snow Country Bike Shop, Parkway Plaza, NY 5 and US 20, Canandaigua (585-394-1530)

—Updated by Jon and Harriett Rubins

9

Canadice and Hemlock Lakes

- **DISTANCE:** 29 miles; moderate to strenuous cycling
- **TERRAIN:** Rolling to hilly terrain
- **COUNTY MAPS:** Livingston, Ontario

This tour circles the two most rustic of the Finger Lakes—the only ones with no cottages, marinas, restaurants, parks, or other development. Except for about 4 miles on state highways, riding is on back roads with little traffic. Sites of historic or cultural interest are few; this ride is largely for the pure pleasure of country riding in a sparsely settled countryside—occasionally it can seem eerily lonely. Toward the end of the tour, a stop at a winery makes a pleasant return to "civilization." The most strenuous part of the tour involves a steep descent into the village of Springwater and an almost equally steep climb out again. Four miles are on unpaved roads, and elsewhere paving is sometimes rough.

The tour starts in the village of Hemlock, at the north end of Hemlock Lake.

0.0 Leave the village of Hemlock by riding south on NY 15A and US 20A. Continue straight on NY 15A just out of town as US 20A goes to the left. *This quiet backwater was once a bustling area of three villages with lumber and flour mills, distilleries, and a potash factory. Hemlock village was known as Slab-City because settlers' houses were made of wood slabs. As this tour goes through a sparsely settled region, you should carry food with you. Hemlock has the small Sugar Creek convenience store, but it might be better to bring supplies from home.*

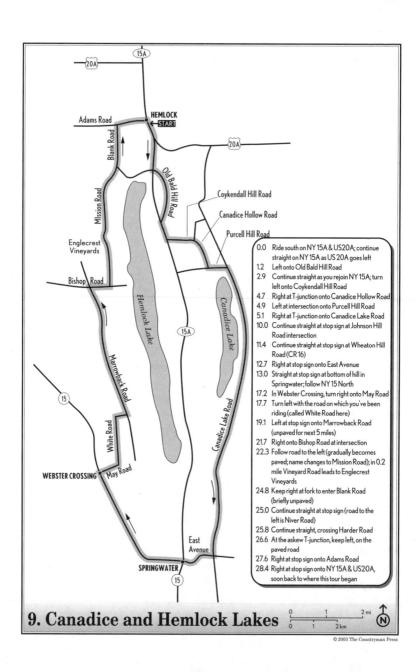

0.0	Ride south on NY 15A & US 20A; continue straight on NY 15A as US 20A goes left
1.2	Left onto Old Bald Hill Road
2.9	Continue straight as you rejoin NY 15A; turn left onto Coykendall Hill Road
4.7	Right at T-junction onto Canadice Hollow Road
4.9	Left at intersection onto Purcell Hill Road
5.1	Right at T-junction onto Canadice Lake Road
10.0	Continue straight at stop sign at Johnson Hill Road intersection
11.4	Continue straight at stop sign at Wheaton Hill Road (CR 16)
12.7	Right at stop sign onto East Avenue
13.0	Straight at stop sign at bottom of hill in Springwater; follow NY 15 North
17.2	In Webster Crossing, turn right onto May Road
17.7	Turn left with the road on which you've been riding (called White Road here)
19.1	Left at stop sign onto Marrowback Road (unpaved for next 5 miles)
21.7	Right onto Bishop Road at intersection
22.3	Follow road to the left (gradually becomes paved; name changes to Mission Road); in 0.2 mile Vineyard Road leads to Englecrest Vineyards
24.8	Keep right at fork to enter Blank Road (briefly unpaved)
25.0	Continue straight at stop sign (road to the left is Niver Road)
25.8	Continue straight, crossing Harder Road
26.6	At the askew T-junction, keep left, on the paved road
27.6	Right at stop sign onto Adams Road
28.4	Right at stop sign onto NY 15A & US 20A, soon back to where this tour began

9. Canadice and Hemlock Lakes

NY 15A has a shoulder and some fast truck traffic, but you ride it for only about a mile.

1.2 Turn left onto Old Bald Hill Road.

2.9 Continue straight, south, as you rejoin NY 15A. In 0.2 mile, turn left onto Coykendall Hill Road.

4.7 At the T-junction, turn right onto Canadice Hollow Road.

4.9 At the intersection, turn left onto Purcell Hill Road.

5.1 Turn right at the T-junction onto Canadice Lake Road.
We can only guess at the Native American sense of humor in naming the shortest of the Finger Lakes Shenadice, or "Long Lake." Three-mile-long Canadice is also the highest of the lakes, at 1,099 feet above sea level, and the most pristine in appearance—hardly an artifact of modern life is seen from its waters, and a scent of conifers along its shore enhances the feeling of being far from civilization.

A mile and eight-tenths along Canadice Lake Road you'll see a rutted dirt road to the right that gives access to the lakeshore. You'll also see NO TRESPASSING signs, intended to protect the lake from degradation, since Canadice, along with its neighbor Hemlock, is part of the city of Rochester's water supply system. Swimming is not permitted in the lake; fishing is allowed with a special free permit, used in conjunction with a regular state fishing license. Small boats, powerless or with motors of up to 7 horsepower, are allowed, again by special permit.

While Canadice and Hemlock Lakes look today somewhat as they must have before settlement by whites, it is surprising to learn that they were not always so. Actually, they have become progressively more rustic as the city of Rochester has gained more control over the watershed. The first water was piped north to the city in 1876, and a second conduit was built in 1893–94. Before that time Hemlock Lake had more than one hundred cottages, five hotels, and five steamboats. The last of the cottages were removed shortly before World War II. Today Canadice and Hemlock supply about one-third of Rochester's water needs.

10.0 Continue straight at the stop sign at the Johnson Hill Road intersection.

11.4 Continue straight at the stop sign at Wheaton Hill Road (also known as CR 16).
On the left after the stop sign is the small Ford Cemetery. Toward the rear is the grave of a veteran of the Revolutionary War, one Pvt. Elisha Capron, once

MARK ROTH

Canadice Lake is the highest and most rustic of the Finger Lakes. Because the lake is a reservoir for the city of Rochester, only small boats are allowed.

a soldier in Colonel Tupper's Massachusetts Regiment.

Two miles east of here is Tabor Hill (elevation 2,244 feet), one of the highest points in the Finger Lakes region.

12.7 Turn right at the stop sign, onto East Avenue.
Before starting down the hill, look back north from this corner. The lake you see is Hemlock; Canadice is hidden to the right. Between them Bald Hill rises to 1,845 feet.

Caution is in order on the downhill that begins here, since it drops more than 500 feet in less than 1 mile. The grade becomes steeper as you descend. Dirt and gravel make the surface slippery. Sit well back on the saddle to get as much weight as possible over the rear wheel, which will discourage it from skidding. And don't hesitate to walk down if you doubt your brakes.

13.0 At the stop sign at the bottom of the hill in Springwater, go straight, following NY 15 North toward Livonia.
The valley village of Springwater has a grocery and luncheonette, antiques shops, and a secondhand bookstore well known to area collectors. The climb from the vil-

lage lasts about 0.75 mile. Riding NY 15 is unavoidable, but it does have a climbing lane for the hill and a good, wide shoulder thereafter.

17.2 In the hamlet of Webster Crossing, turn right onto May Road, opposite the church.

17.7 Turn left with the road on which you've been riding, here called White Road.
This is quite a long, strenuous climb.

19.1 Turn left at the stop sign onto Marrowback Road. From here the road is unpaved for the next 5 miles.
Marrowback Hill reaches 1,940 feet, and the road is almost that high. The valley to the east contains Hemlock Lake, though the lake itself won't be visible for some time yet.

21.7 Turn right onto Bishop Road at the intersection. This is the first right turn possible.

22.3 Follow the road to the left as it gradually becomes paved and its name changes to Mission Road. (Do not enter the dead end straight ahead.) In 0.2 mile Vineyard Road, to the right, takes you to the Englecrest Vineyards.
The O-Neh-Da Vineyard was started on this site by Bishop Bernard McQuaid of Rochester in 1872 to make sacramental wine. The name comes from the Native American word for hemlock, and it was their name for the lake. In 1924 it was purchased by the Society of the Divine Word, whose large seminary you'll pass about 0.5 mile north of the winery.

24.8 Keep right at the fork to enter Blank Road, which is briefly unpaved.

25.0 Continue straight at the stop sign. Here the road to the left is Niver Road.

25.8 Continue straight, crossing Harder Road.

26.6 At the askew T-junction, keep left, on the paved road.

27.6 Turn right at the stop sign onto Adams Road.

28.4 Turn right at the stop sign onto NY 15A and US 20A. Soon you'll be back where this tour began.

Bicycle Shops
Snow Country Bike Shop, Parkway Plaza, NY 5 and US 20, Canandaigua (585-394-1530)

Swain Ski & Sports, 131 Main Street, Geneseo (585-243-0832)

—Updated by Michael Priestman

10

Genesee Valley and Gorge

- **DISTANCE:** 57 miles; easy to strenuous cycling
- **TERRAIN:** Varied terrain; flat stretches and both gradual and steep hills
- **COUNTY MAP:** Livingston

One of the first Europeans to see the Genesee Valley described it as "the most beautiful flats I ever saw, being not less than 4 miles in width, and extending from right to left as far as can be seen." This tour passes through that valley and along the 17-mile length of the spectacular Genesee River Gorge in Letchworth State Park. Strong cyclists can do the ride in a day, though the first third of the ride is deceptively easy compared with the rest. Pushing to finish in one day would be a mistake for leisurely cyclists; there's enough to see to repay fully spending two—or more—days on this route.

Overnight accommodations are available just short of the halfway point at the Genesee Falls Inn in Portageville, which charges $55–$125 for two. As there is no other place to stay in Portageville, reservations are suggested (call 585-493-2484). Overnight facilities in Letchworth State Park include tent and trailer campsites, log cabins, and inn accommodations. In summer Letchworth is very popular, and reservations are essential. Campsites and cabins can be reserved through Ticketmaster, or by writing or calling Letchworth State Park, Castile 14427 (585-493-3600). To stay at the park's Glen Iris Inn, write in care of the above address, or call 585-493-2622.

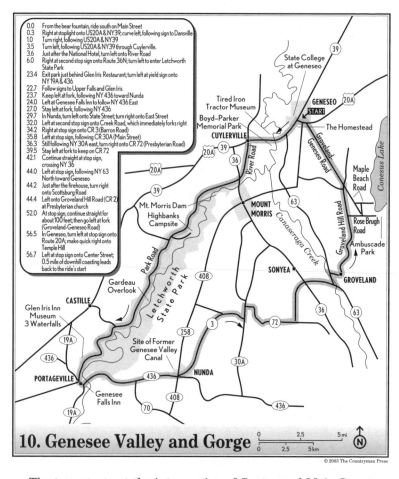

0.0	From the bear fountain, ride south on Main Street
0.3	Right at stoplight onto US20A & NY39; curve left, following sign to Dansville
1.0	Turn right, following US20A & NY39
3.5	Turn left, following US20A & NY39 through Cuylerville.
3.6	Just after the National Hotel, turn left onto River Road
6.0	Right at second stop sign onto Route 36N; turn left to enter Letchworth State Park
23.4	Exit park just behind Glen Iris Restaurant; turn left at yield sign onto NY 19A & 436
22.7	Follow signs to Upper Falls and Glen Iris
23.7	Keep left at fork, following NY 436 toward Nunda
24.0	Left at Genesee Falls Inn to follow NY 436 East
27.0	Stay left at fork, following NY 436
29.7	In Nunda, turn left onto State Street; turn right onto East Street
32.0	Left at second stop sign onto Creek Road, which immediately forks right
34.2	Right at stop sign onto CR 3 (Barron Road)
35.8	Left at stop sign, following CR 30A (Main Street)
36.3	Still following NY 30A east, turn right onto CR 72 (Presbyterian Road)
39.5	Stay left at fork to keep on CR 72
42.1	Continue straight at stop sign, crossing NY 36
44.0	Left at stop sign, following NY 63 North toward Geneseo
44.2	Just after the firehouse, turn right onto Scottsburg Road
44.4	Left onto Groveland Hill Road (CR 2) at Presbyterian church
52.0	At stop sign, continue straight for about 100 feet; then go left at fork (Groveland-Geneseo Road)
56.5	In Geneseo, turn left at stop sign onto Route 20A; make quick right onto Temple Hill
56.7	Left at stop sign onto Center Street; 0.5 mile of downhill coasting leads back to the ride's start

10. Genesee Valley and Gorge

© 2003 The Countryman Press

The tour starts at the intersection of Center and Main Streets in the village of Geneseo.

0.0 From the bear fountain (in the center of Main Street), ride south on Main Street so that the college and the Genesee River are to your right.

When the weary men of General Sullivan's 1779 expedition against the Iroquois finally saw the Genesee Valley, their farmers' eyes must have widened. Diaries acclaim "a very beautiful flat of great extent growing up with grass higher than our heads . . . the land can't be equaled . . . undoubtedly the best land, and capable of the greatest improvement, of any part of the possessions of the U. States."

The Genesee Valley did soon become the breadbasket of the nation, with Rochester the leading flour-milling city in the world. Almost two hundred years after its sod first felt the plow, thousands of acres are still owned by the Wadsworth family, descendants of the first pioneers. Wadsworths have been farmers and congressmen, generals, senators, and ambassadors. Two branches of the family still live at either end of Geneseo's Main Street. In autumn the Wadsworth-initiated Genesee Valley Hunt rides cross-country after the fox.

Since 1871 there has been a state college in Geneseo. The modern buildings of the State University College cling to the hillside, affording a grand view of the Genesee Valley.

Groceries can be bought in Geneseo and in most of the towns on this route; there is also a store in the Highbanks campsite of Letchworth Park.

0.3 Turn right at the stoplight onto US 20A and NY 39. In 100 yards curve left, following the sign to Dansville.
To your left are the grounds of the Wadsworth estate known as The Homestead.

1.0 Turn right, still following US 20A and NY 39 and a sign to Letchworth State Park.
In less than a mile you'll cross the Genesee River, and a mile beyond that you'll come to the Boyd-Parker Memorial Park. The park borders the site of a large Seneca Indian village called Genesee Castle, or Little Beard's Town. General Sullivan followed Washington's orders and destroyed the town, yet his official report sounds almost regretful: "The Castle consisted of 128 houses mostly large and elegant. The place was beautifully situated, almost encircled with a cleared flat, which extended for a number of miles, where the most extensive fields of corn were waving, and every kind of vegetable that can be conceived." The unlucky Thomas Boyd and Michael Parker, scouts sent out by Sullivan, were here tortured to death by their Indian captors on September 13, 1779. The next day Sullivan leveled the town, buried his men, and turned the army back east. They needed to go no farther; the Senecas had been destroyed.

The Boyd-Parker Park has picnic tables, rest rooms, and pump water. Across the road is the Tired Iron Tractor Museum, where old farm machinery can be seen on Sunday 11 AM–6 PM, May through October. Admission is $2.

3.5 Turn left, following US 20A and NY 39 through Cuylerville.

The Tired Iron Tractor Museum displays old farm machinery in the flat, agriculturally rich Genesee Valley.

3.6 Just after the National Hotel, turn left onto River Road.
Flat, straight River Road parallels railroad tracks built on a filled section of the financially unsuccessful Genesee Valley Canal, begun in 1836 but abandoned in 1878.

6.0 Turn right at the second stop sign onto NY 36N, and in 50 feet turn left to enter Letchworth State Park.
In about 2 miles an overlook gives a spectacular view of the Mount Morris Dam and the almost 500-foot-deep canyon exposing some 400 million years of geologic history. Park features include many overlooks of the river canyon, snack bars, restaurants, swimming pools, and hiking trails. About 6 miles into the park is the Highbanks campsite, open from early May to early October.

Some 5 miles past Highbanks is the Gardeau Overlook, with an expansive view of lands once homesteaded by Mary Jemison, the "White Woman of the Genesee." As a girl, Mary was adopted by Native Americans who had killed the rest of her family in a frontier raid. For the next three-quarters of a century she lived as a Genesee. She received title to more than 17,000 acres around Gardeau at the Treaty of Big Tree in 1797, where she acted as interpreter for the tribe. Thomas Morris, representing his father, Robert, was so worried that negotiations for Native American land would fall through without Mary's help that he agreed to give her the immensely valuable holding. The Treaty of Big Tree was finally signed by 52 Native Americans; among them were Hot Bread, Parrot Nose, and To-Destroy-a-Town.

22.7 Follow signs to Upper Falls and Glen Iris.
In 1859 a rich bachelor named William Pryor Letchworth bought Glen Iris and 1,000 acres around it as a summer retreat; for the next half century, preserving the whole Genesee Gorge, including the three fabulous waterfalls nearby, became his passion. The nucleus of the present park came into state ownership upon Letchworth's death in 1910. The museum near the Glen Iris Inn has exhibits about Letchworth, Mary Jemison, and local Native American and pioneer history. The grave of Mary Jemison and a Seneca longhouse can be seen on the plateau above the museum. The Glen Iris Inn restaurant is open daily at mealtimes; guest rooms (within hearing distance of thundering Middle Falls) rent from $80 for a double and are usually booked.

Geologists believe that the three great falls along this section of the river were formed as the ice sheet receded intermittently, lowering the water level and exposing new sections to downcutting. The 1852 railroad bridge over the Upper Falls was a major tourist attraction—the largest wooden bridge in the world—until it burned in 1875. In two months it was replaced by the iron bridge that is still standing. For more information, log on to the Glen Iris Inn web site, www.glenirisinn.com.

23.4 Exit the park just behind Glen Iris Restaurant, at the Portageville exit, and turn left at the yield sign onto NY 19A and 436.

23.7 Keep left at the fork, following NY 436 toward Nunda.

24.0 At the Genesee Falls Inn, turn left to follow NY 436 East across the Genesee River.
The Genesee Falls Inn is the only 19th-century tavern-inn remaining from the busy days of train excursions to see the wondrous bridge 250 feet above the raging river.

A steep climb of 0.6 mile brings you up the glacier-formed Valley Heads

Moraine, stretching eastward across the whole Finger Lakes region, preventing the lakes from draining to the south. The moraine is also responsible for the Genesee Gorge; it blocked the Genesee River from its preglacial course, forcing it to excavate the gorge through what is now Letchworth Park.

27.0 Stay left at the fork, following NY 436.
Two and a half miles farther, a sign on the left locates the lowest of 17 locks that once carried the long-abandoned Genesee Valley Canal to Portageville over the hills you just coasted down. The locks can be best seen before foliage is fully out.

29.7 In the village of Nunda, turn left onto State Street. In 200 feet, turn right onto East Street.
Nunda (a Native American word for "hill") has grocery stores and restaurants.

32.0 Turn left at the second stop sign onto Creek Road, which immediately forks to the right.

34.2 Turn right at the stop sign onto CR 3 (Barron Road).

35.8 Turn left at the stop sign, following CR 30A (Main Street).

36.3 Still following CR 30A east, turn right onto CR 72 (Presbyterian Road).

39.5 Stay left at the fork to keep on CR 72.

42.1 Continue straight at the stop sign, crossing NY 36.
The wide valley you cross here holds only tiny Canaseraga Creek, which is much too small to have carved it. Geologists explain that the valley was formed by the Genesee River, which flowed here prior to the Ice Age. Today, the Genesee rejoins its old valley after emerging from the narrow Letchworth Gorge, near Mount Morris.

You may have noted that farmhouses over the last few miles often don't reflect the rich quality of the land. This is because many of the farms are owned by people living elsewhere and are leased to tenants. Livingston County has the highest proportion of tenant farms in the Finger Lakes.

44.0 Turn left at the stop sign, following NY 63 North toward Geneseo.

44.2 Just after the firehouse, turn right onto Scottsburg Road, following a small sign to Groveland Hill.

44.4 Turn left onto Groveland Hill Road, also called CR 2, at the

Presbyterian Church. This stiff uphill lasts more than 2 miles and brings you 750 feet above the valley.

The direct route back to Geneseo continues straight for a few miles.

An alternate route to visit the site of the Groveland Ambuscade, where Boyd and Parker were captured, turns right here. In 1.4 miles a small ambuscade sign points to the right, where you'll find a picnic shelter and water pump. The memorial obelisk is reached by a grass path from the uphill side of the park.

The Sullivan campaign burned Native American villages and crops, but there were few casualties on either side. In terms of lives lost, the battle known as the Groveland Ambuscade was the most costly to the Colonials—14 men were killed on the spot.

A lethal chain of coincidences began on the night of September 12, when General Sullivan, who had only sketchy maps, sent out a scouting party led by Sgt. Thomas Boyd to locate a rich Indian town rumored to be in the Genesee Valley. In darkness Boyd and two dozen or so men crossed the Conesus Lake inlet, climbed Groveland Hill, and continued westward. They found only a small abandoned village. At dawn the patrol turned back east toward the main army, unaware that its path was now blocked by a Tory–Native American force waiting in ambush on Groveland Hill. The slaughter was quick and thorough; only a few flankers escaped. But the firing on Boyd's patrol alerted Sullivan to the enemy's presence. Having lost the advantage of surprise, the Native Americans and the British retreated to Little Beard's Town, with Boyd and Parker as captives. Though they had not intended to be martyrs, the hapless scouting party saved the lives of many men in the main force.

To continue toward Geneseo from the ambuscade site, push back up the hill past Lakeview Cemetery and turn right at the corner onto the paved road (the less sharp right turn). Keep going straight where you join Maple Beach Road. In another mile, turn right at the stop sign, and then left at the fork, with Adamson's store to your right.

52.0 At the stop sign, continue straight for about 100 feet, crossing CR44; then go left at the fork so that the vacant Corner Store is to your right. This is Groveland-Geneseo Road.

56.5 In Geneseo, turn left at the stop sign onto US 20A; make a quick right in 30 feet onto Temple Hill.

The brick Georgian mansion in the landscaped grounds to the left was built in 1827 by James Wadsworth as an academy, or high school. Many of the schools in the Finger Lakes are still referred to as academies. To staff it he hired three young Harvard graduates, one of whom, Cornelius C. Felton, was later president of that university.

56.7 Turn left at the stop sign onto Center Street. A half mile of downhill coasting will bring you back where the ride began.

Those wanting to know more about local history can visit the Livingston County Historical Museum at 30 Center Street. The museum, housed in an 1838 cobblestone school building, is open Thursday and Sunday 2–5 PM in May, June, September, and October, and Tuesday 2–5 PM in July and August.

Geneseo's famed Big Tree Inn is at 46 Main Street (585-243-5220). The handsome 1833 Federal-style house was converted from a private dwelling to an inn by a Wadsworth scion in 1885. Today no lodging is offered, but gourmet lunches and dinners are served Monday through Saturday; an abundant "country breakfast buffet" is prepared 10 AM–2 PM on Sunday. In the taproom, food is available daily 9 AM–2 PM and 5–9 PM. Dinners average about $20.

Nearby Bed-and-Breakfasts

Conesus Lake B&B, 2388 East Lake Road, Conesus (585-346-6526)

MacPhail House B&B, 5477 Lakeville Road, Geneseo (585-346-5600)

Meadowood Acres, 6628 Denton Corners Road, Castile (585-493-2940)

Oak Valley Inn, 4235 Lakeville Road, Geneseo (585-243-5570)

Perry B&B, 9 North Federal, Perry (585-237-6289)

Bicycle Shops

Swain Ski & Sports, 131 Main Street, Geneseo (585-243-0832)

—Updated by John and Cathy Van Vechten

11

Pittsford–Erie Canal

- **DISTANCE:** 19 miles; easy to moderate cycling
- **TERRAIN:** Flat canal towpath and low hilly terrain
- **COUNTY MAP:** Monroe

Affluent suburbs often have a sameness that makes them hard to distinguish, and a blandness that makes the effort barely worthwhile. The Rochester suburb of Pittsford has a standard shopping center, but it also has some of the best old buildings in western New York, a quaint village center, working farms, and a restored towpath along the Barge Canal, which here follows the route of the original Erie. Pittsford antedates nearby Rochester by almost a quarter century and has a long list of area firsts: sawmill, schoolhouse, library, post office, newspaper. The Erie Canal enlivened Pittsford, but it created Rochester.

The significance of the Erie Canal is hard to appreciate today, when airplanes and the interstate highway system, for example, are mere supplements to other means of transportation. But for years the Erie was almost the only way through a wilderness scarred by scarcely a mud track. Men with shovels and wheelbarrows piled up dirt for four years to build the embankment you ride on between Bushnells Basin and Pittsford. More than 4 miles of canal-side riding on the gravel towpath give you a level path and a view you can imagine sharing with old-time "canawlers." Away from the towpath, the route winds through a region of working and genteel farms and passes through a vast county park with ponds

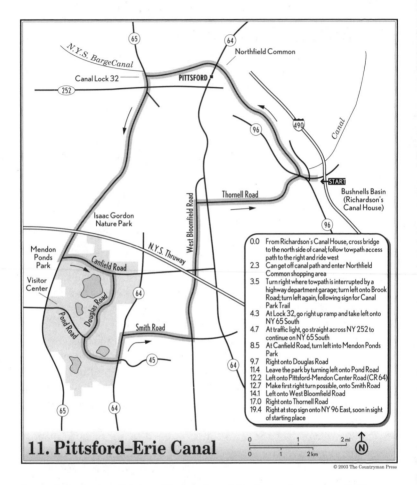

N.Y.S. BargeCanal

Canal Lock 32

252

PITTSFORD

Northfield Common

Canal

490

96

Thornell Road

START

Bushnells Basin
(Richardson's
Canal House)

96

Isaac Gordon
Nature Park

West Bloomfield Road

N.Y.S. Thruway

Mendon
Ponds
Park

Canfield Road

Visitor
Center

64

Douglas Road

Pond Road

Smith Road

45

64

65

64

0.0	From Richardson's Canal House, cross bridge to the north side of canal; follow towpath access path to the right and ride west
2.3	Can get off canal path and enter Northfield Common shopping area
3.5	Turn right where towpath is interrupted by a highway department garage; turn left onto Brook Road; turn left again, following sign for Canal Park Trail
4.3	At Lock 32, go right up ramp and take left onto NY 65 South
4.7	At traffic light, go straight across NY 252 to continue on NY 65 South
8.5	At Canfield Road, turn left into Mendon Ponds Park
9.7	Right onto Douglas Road
11.4	Leave the park by turning left onto Pond Road
12.2	Left onto Pittsford-Mendon Center Road (CR 64)
12.7	Make first right turn possible, onto Smith Road
14.1	Left onto West Bloomfield Road
17.0	Right onto Thornell Road
19.4	Right at stop sign onto NY 96 East, soon in sight of starting place

11. Pittsford–Erie Canal

0   1   2 mi
0   1   2 km

N

© 2003 The Countryman Press

for swimming or fishing. Convenient bike rentals are available from Towpath Bike Shop at the Northfield Common in Pittsford.

The tour starts at Bushnells Basin, on the Barge Canal some 2 miles southeast of Pittsford village, near the Bushnells Basin exit of NY 490.

0.0 From the front of Richardson's Canal House, cross the bridge to the north side of the canal; then, just over the bridge, at the break in the guardrail, follow the towpath access path to the right. On the gravel towpath ride west, so that the canal is to your left.

Richardson's Canal House is perhaps the oldest canal-side tavern surviving from the heyday of the old Erie Canal. Built in 1818 and first managed by brothers named Richardson, it was not a fancy inn; canallers came there to engage in drinking and brawling that soon became legendary, and to sleep on the floor. The menu, a creative blend of Continental and American cuisines, changes seasonally to take advantage of various fresh fruits and vegetables as they reach their peak. Dinner reservations are advisable (585-248-5000). Next door, eight rooms accommodate guests at the Oliver Loud's Inn.

From Bushnells Basin to Pittsford village the canal is carried over the Irondequoit Valley on a man-made ridge called the Great Embankment. Heaping it up required a massive effort by men, mules, and oxen. For two of the embankment's four construction years the great canal ended at the wide waters of Bushnells Basin, and Richardson's (or simply the West End Tavern) was an especially busy place. As you might guess as you ride along the Great Embankment high above the surrounding countryside, a breach in the canal here could cause great damage. In the early years even so much as a muskrat burrowing in the earth banks could empty the canal and flood the neighborhood.

Those who want to carry food along can shop at the Hitching Post Plaza, across from the Canal House, or in Pittsford village, which also has several restaurants.

2.3 Here you can get off the canal path and enter the Northfield Common shopping area.

Northfield's former industrial and warehouse buildings, once serving canal and railroad, were adapted to crafts shops, boutiques, and restaurants in the 1970s. This may be one of your few opportunities to eat in an old coal tower. There is also a bike shop, which has rentals.

For a diversion to see some of Pittsford village, ascend to street level and cross the bridge over the canal. A pleasant canal-side park is to the left immediately across the bridge. Continuing straight, at the traffic light you'll see the old redbrick Phoenix Hotel building. Now occupied by several businesses, this harmonious Federal-style building dates from 1807, about 20 years after the first settlers arrived.

From the early days, Pittsford produced and attracted wealth with milling, farming, quarrying, small manufacturing, and legal, medical, and canal-related services; later, its charm and proximity to Rochester made it a choice for country estates.

Cyclists, runners, and walkers enjoy miles of traffic-free quiet on the paths that run alongside the Erie Canal.

Some of Pittsford's best houses can be seen if you turn right, west, onto Monroe Avenue (NY 31) for a block or two. (It is best to walk on the sidewalk here as traffic is often heavy.) The older buildings date from the late Federal period, roughly 1815 to 1830. The local historical society occupies the small former lawyer's office on the right. Other village streets are worth exploring, if you have time. A row of 19th-century commercial buildings can be seen across Main Street from the Phoenix Hotel.

3.5 As the towpath is interrupted by a highway department garage, you must turn right. About 200 feet farther, turn left onto Brook Road. In approximately another 200 yards, turn left, following a sign for the Canal Park Trail at the yellow gate.

4.3 At Lock #32, just at the bridge, go right up the ramp and take a left onto NY 65 South. (Care is needed in crossing the bridge over the canal as there is no shoulder.)
From Lock #32, canal traffic going west has only one more lock to negotiate before entering the Long Level, 63 uninterrupted miles with "neither lock, block, nor stay to traffic" all the way to Lockport. In all, the present Barge Canal has 35 locks, less than

half the number the Erie needed to bridge the 570-foot drop from Lake Erie to the Hudson River. On the west side of NY 65 you can stop and take a rest at the lock.

4.7 At the traffic light, go straight across NY 252 to continue on NY 65 South.
The wide shoulder of NY 65 is marked as a bike path, and motor traffic should lessen as you proceed south. In about 3 miles, shortly before crossing over the New York State Thruway, you'll see the Isaac Gordon Nature Park on your left. A shaded main trail leads to two loops: The Hardwood Trail branches to the right, and the Pond Trail descends to the left. About a half hour should be allowed for walking either trail; each has a picnic table.

8.5 At Canfield Road, turn left into Mendon Ponds Park (at the crest of a small hill).

9.7 Turn right onto Douglas Road.
The ponds in this 550-acre park are excellent for swimming or fishing, and picnic tables, grills, and rest rooms are provided.

The park contains a variety of glacial features such as moraines, eskers, kames, and kettle holes. Diagrams and photos in the Mendon Ponds Nature Center explain these interesting surface features and other aspects of local natural history. Self-guiding nature trails radiate from the center; feeding stations along them are usually successful in luring birds within easy view. The center can be reached by calling 585-334-3780. To go to the center, do not exit the park as described below, but continue straight on Pond Road for about a mile.

11.4 Leave the park by turning left onto Pond Road.

12.2 Turn left onto Pittsford–Mendon Center Road (CR 64).

12.7 Make the first right turn possible, onto Smith Road.

14.1 Turn left onto West Bloomfield Road.

17.0 Turn right onto Thornell Road.
Thornell Road is straight for a while, and then it twists as if designed by someone who hated cartographers. Despite the twists, clear signposting should allow you to stay on Thornell with little confusion.

19.4 At the stop sign, turn right onto NY 96 East. In a couple of hundred feet you'll be in sight of your starting place at Bushnells Basin.

Nearby Bed-and-Breakfasts

Oliver Loud's Inn, 1474 Marsh Road, Pittsford (585-248-5200)

Bicycle Shops

Recreational Vehicles & Equipment, 40 North Main Street, Fairport (585-388-1350)

Towpath Bike Shop, 7 Schoen Place, Pittsford (585-381-2808)

—Updated by Peter Bud

12

East Bloomfield–Powder Mills Park

- **DISTANCE:** 32 miles; moderate cycling
- **TERRAIN:** Small hills with only a few level places
- **COUNTY MAPS:** Monroe, Ontario

Although this route comes within 7 miles of the Rochester city limits, it is a rural ride through attractive farm- and woodland. You'll visit a neat country village with an antique radio museum, pass an extensive orchard of easy-to-pick dwarf apple trees (bearing some of the largest apples you'll ever see), and traverse a spacious county park with a trout hatchery.

In 1687, the Marquis de Denonville, then governor of New France with headquarters in Québec, decided that the Native Americans had become "exalted to a tone of insolence that must be brought down." He was annoyed by their interference with the French fur trade and affronted at their resistance to French Jesuit missionaries. Attacking with fifteen hundred Frenchmen and five hundred Native American allies, Denonville wiped out four Seneca villages south and east of present-day Rochester. The sites of two of these villages are passed on this tour.

The ride starts at Elton Park, also known as the green in the village of East Bloomfield, on NY 5 and US 20.

0.0 Begin by riding north (downhill) along the green's west side, the side facing the East Bloomfield Academy.

An 1845 newspaper advertisement for the East Bloomfield Academy promised instruction in English, higher mathematics, Greek, piano, French, German, practical

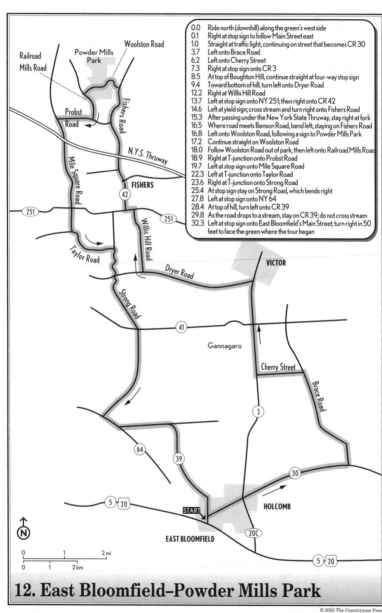

0.0	Ride north (downhill) along the green's west side
0.1	Right at stop sign to follow Main Street east
1.0	Straight at traffic light, continuing on street that becomes CR 30
3.7	Left onto Brace Road
6.2	Left onto Cherry Street
7.3	Right at stop sign onto CR 3
8.5	At top of Boughton Hill, continue straight at four-way stop sign
9.4	Toward bottom of hill, turn left onto Dryer Road
12.2	Right at Willis Hill Road
13.7	Left at stop sign onto NY 251; then right onto CR 42
14.6	Left at yield sign; cross stream and turn right onto Fishers Road
15.3	After passing under the New York State Thruway, stay right at fork
16.5	Where road meets Benson Road, bend left, staying on Fishers Road
16.8	Left onto Woolston Road, following a sign to Powder Mills Park
17.2	Continue straight on Woolston Road
18.0	Follow Woolston Road out of park, then left onto Railroad Mills Road
18.9	Right at T-junction onto Probst Road
19.7	Left at stop sign onto Mile Square Road
22.3	Left at T-junction onto Taylor Road
23.6	Right at T-junction onto Strong Road
25.4	At stop sign stay on Strong Road, which bends right
27.8	Left at stop sign onto NY 64
28.4	At top of hill, turn left onto CR 39
29.8	As the road drops to a stream, stay on CR 39; do not cross stream
32.3	Left at stop sign onto East Bloomfield's Main Street; turn right in 50 feet to face the green where the tour began

Railroad Mills Road

Powder Mills Park

Woolston Road

Fishers Road

Probst Road

Mile Square Road

N.Y.S. Thruway

FISHERS

42

251

Willis Hill Road

251

Taylor Road

Strong Road

Dryer Road

VICTOR

41

Gannagaro

Cherry Street

Brace Road

3

64

39

30

5 20

START

HOLCOMB

N

0   1   2 mi

0   1   2 km

EAST BLOOMFIELD

20C

5 20

12. East Bloomfield–Powder Mills Park

surveying, and civil engineering. Today its handsome brick building houses the East Bloomfield Historical Society and the museum of the Antique Wireless Association, with displays that represent pioneering efforts in telegraph, telephone, phonograph, and television. A wall of the museum is stocked as a radio store would have been in 1925, when radio was a do-it-yourself hobby. No admission is charged, and the museum is open May 1 through October 31, Sunday 2–5 PM and Wednesday 7–9 PM. The historical society's side of the building is open from Memorial Day to Christmas, Wednesday through Saturday 1–4 PM, plus the hours that the radio museum is open. To the left of the entrance you can find students' names incised in the brick facade along with 19th-century dates—when, we can guess, the graffiti artists were hidden by shrubs.

Across NY 5 and US 20 from the Congregational church is Holloway House, a tavern and coaching inn dating from 1808. As no grocery stores are convenient, it is best to bring food with you.

0.1 Turn right at the stop sign to follow Main Street east.

1.0 Go straight at the traffic light, continuing on the street that becomes CR 30.

A historical marker on the left near Mud Creek commemorates the site of Gandagourae, a Seneca Indian village destroyed in the French raid. The Jesuits at the Saint Michel Mission here were recalled shortly before the raid was scheduled.

3.7 Turn left onto Brace Road.

6.2 Turn left onto Cherry Street.

7.3 At the stop sign, turn right onto CR 3.

8.5 At the top of Boughton Hill, continue straight at the four-way stop sign.

Just before the intersection, a marker in the shape of a cross identifies the site of Gannagaro, once the Seneca capital, with perhaps seven thousand inhabitants. It was the summer of 1687 that Denonville marched on Gannagaro; his report summarized events: "On the next day, 14th July, we marched to one of the large villages where we encamped. We found it burned and a fort quite nigh; it was very advantageously situated on a hill. I deem it our best policy to employ ourselves laying waste the Indian corn which was in vast abundance in the fields, rather than follow a flying enemy to a distance and excite our troops to catch only some straggling fugitives." Though the French soon departed, Gannagaro was not reoccupied by the Native Americans; instead they drifted east toward Canandaigua and Geneva. The raid earned the French the lasting hatred of the Senecas, and it led the whole Iroquois Confederacy to side with the English in the wars of the 18th century.

On the left, just after the intersection, is a good example of a house in the Italianate style, popular between 1840 and 1880, characterized by wide eaves supported by large brackets, tall windows, a low-pitched hip roof, and double doors with glass panels. In 1986 this house, the nearby meetinghouse, and surrounding land were acquired by the Office of Parks, Recreation and Historic Preservation. Exhibits in the circa-1830 meetinghouse recount the story of early Native American settlement in the area.

9.4 Toward the bottom of the hill, turn left onto Dryer Road.
Two and a half miles farther, where Malone Road enters, are two good cobblestone buildings. The one closer to the road was built as a school in 1834.

12.2 Turn right at Willis Hill Road.

13.7 At the stop sign, turn left onto NY 251 for about 150 yards; then turn right onto CR 42, following the sign to Fishers.

14.6 At the yield sign, turn left; cross the stream, and turn right onto Fishers Road.
For a look at the hamlet of Fishers (formerly Fishers Station, a stop on the Auburn and Rochester Railroad), turn right instead of left at the yield sign. In 100 or so yards on the right is a small cobblestone pump house. Built in 1845, it is said to be the second oldest surviving railroad building in the country. (The oldest is in Baltimore.)

15.3 After passing under the New York State Thruway, stay to the right at the fork.

16.5 Where your road meets Benson Road, bend left, staying on the paved Fishers Road, with the pond to your right.

16.8 Turn left onto Woolston Road, following a sign to Powder Mills Park.

17.2 Continue straight on Woolston Road, as a park road enters from the right.
The name Powder Mills recalls the gunpowder factories once here. The powder was shipped by wagon to Bushnells Basin, there to be loaded aboard barges on the Erie Canal. Signs at this corner note various park attractions. To see the trout hatchery you turn right here; to fish for the trout, continue straight and in about a half mile you'll come to a small stream stocked with trout—and anglers. The 576-

The 1845 cobblestone pump house at Fishers once served trains of the Auburn and Rochester Railroad.

acre park is perfect for a lunch or refreshment break. It has picnic tables, drinking water, and rest rooms.

18.0 After following Woolston Road out of the park, make a left turn of about 160 degrees onto Railroad Mills Road.

18.9 At the T-junction, turn right onto Probst Road.

19.7 Turn left at the stop sign onto Mile Square Road.

22.3 Turn left at the T-junction onto Taylor Road.

23.6 Turn right at the T-junction onto Strong Road.
Many of the small hills you ride over and around here are kames, formed in temporary lakes created by glacial damming and melting. Streams flowing into the lakes carried the sand and gravel of which the kames are composed.

25.4 At the stop sign, stay on Strong Road, which bends about 20 degrees to the right.

27.8 Turn left at the stop sign onto NY 64.

28.4 At the top of the hill, turn left onto CR 39.

29.8 As the road drops to a stream, stay on CR 39, which here makes a 90-degree turn to the right. Do not cross the stream.

32.3 At the stop sign, turn left onto East Bloomfield's Main Street. In about 50 feet turn right, and you'll be facing the green where the tour began.

Nearby Bed-and-Breakfasts

Safari House B&B Deluxe, 950 Deer Crossing, Victor (585-924-0250)

Woods Edge, 151 Bluhm Road, Fairport (585-223-8877)

Bicycle Shops

Snow Country Bike Shop, Parkway Plaza, NY 5 and US 20, Canandaigua (585-394-1530)

Towpath Bike Shop, 7 Schoen Place, Pittsford (585-381-2808)

—Updated by Rob Clark

13

Mormon Country

- **DISTANCE:** 29 miles; moderate cycling
- **TERRAIN:** Low, rolling (drumlin) hills
- **COUNTY MAPS:** Ontario, Wayne

Geologists come from far away to see the hills you'll be riding around and over on this tour. Between Lake Ontario and the Finger Lakes there are perhaps ten thousand drumlins—the largest such concentration in the world. Simply, drumlins are glacially formed hills shaped somewhat like an egg cut in half lengthwise. Generally less than 200 feet high, they are long from north to south, the direction of glacial flow, and steep and narrow from east to west. Cycling here you'll find that the vistas change constantly, as must your gear selection. After a few miles of east–west riding, you'll likely have new respect for 200-foot-high hills.

One of the few drumlins with a name is Hill Cumorah, or Mormon Hill. It was here that Joseph Smith claimed to have received the golden plates of the Book of Mormon, sacred to the Church of Jesus Christ of Latter-Day Saints. As geologists come for the drumlins, thousands of Mormons make pilgrimages to Hill Cumorah, Joseph Smith's home, the Sacred Grove, and Martin Harris's farm—all of which are passed on this tour. In addition, the ride passes the birthplace of modern spiritualism, a coverlet museum, and a canal park where you can see both the old Erie Canal and the modern Barge Canal. Fishing is possible along the route.

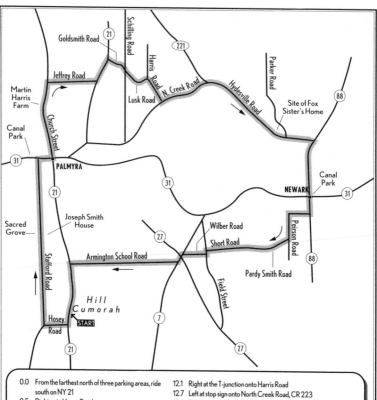

13. Mormon Country

This ride does not begin near food stores, so you may want to bring supplies with you. Both Palmyra and Newark along your route later on have groceries and restaurants.

The tour starts at the parking area of Hill Cumorah, on NY 21, 4 miles south of the village of Palmyra. (*Note:* During the Mormon Pageant, parking here is by permit only; then the tour can be started in Palmyra.)

0.0 From the farthest north of three parking areas, ride south on NY 21, so that Hill Cumorah is to your left.

Hill Cumorah is a 683-foot-high drumlin; to its slopes the young Joseph Smith was directed by the Angel Moroni, son of Mormon, in 1823. Four years later, after presumably proving worthy, he was allowed to remove the golden plates containing the Book of Mormon from the hill and was inspired with the ability to translate the unknown language in which they were written. According to the Mormons, Hill Cumorah was the site of a fatal battle between peoples called Nephites and Lamanites in a.d. 420. The Hill Cumorah Pageant, held each year toward the middle of July, recounts this conflict, as well as other events important to Mormons. The outdoor performances start at 9 PM, and admission is free. For details, call 315-597-5851.

0.5 Turn right onto Hosey Road.

1.2 At the T-junction, turn right onto Stafford Road.

Here riding is between long, low drumlins—much easier than riding east-west over them.

In about 2.5 miles you'll come to the Joseph Smith House. The house was started by the Smiths in 1822 and occupied by Joseph, his parents, and his seven siblings from 1825 to 1828. Some of the Book of Mormon was translated here. Apart from this historic connection, the house has interesting period furnishings and implements. Tours are free; some proselytizing may be encountered.

Across the road from the house is what Mormons call the Sacred Grove, where, in 1820, Joseph Smith is supposed to have first seen the Angel Moroni. Yearly meetings followed each September from 1823 to 1827, when the golden plates were entrusted to Smith. The Sacred Grove and the path to it are nicely landscaped and quite pretty.

3.0 Bear left at the fork to remain on Stafford Road (unsignposted).

5.1 Entering the village of Palmyra, proceed straight on Stafford Street.

5.6 At the intersection with NY 31, Main Street, turn right (east).
If you ride west instead for about 0.25 mile, you can visit the largest canal park along the state's waterway system, with picnic tables, rest rooms, and drinking water. This is also the most convenient place to compare the old Erie Canal with its modern Barge Canal successor; standing in one spot, you can watch boats passing through Lock #29 and see an aqueduct built in 1856 that once carried the Erie over Ganargua (Mud) Creek. The creek is a popular fishing spot.

6.0 At the corner with the four churches, turn left onto Church Street, here called Canandaigua Street.
If you continue straight on Main Street into Palmyra village, noted for its Victorian architecture and cast-iron storefronts, you'll find groceries and restaurants.

Henry Wells, cofounder of Wells-Fargo Express Company, started his business in Palmyra, delivering small packages on foot in the early 1840s. North of Main Street, at 122 William Street, is the Alling Coverlet Museum, housing the largest collection of coverlets in the country. May through October the museum is open 1–4 PM. Admission is free. For more information, call 315-597-6737.

Palmyra was one of the first towns settled in Wayne County (1789), but it did not flourish until the building of the Erie Canal in the 1820s. This period in its history is treated in the novel Canal Town by Samuel Hopkins Adams. The second weekend after Labor Day each September, Palmyra celebrates its historic relationship with the canal with a long weekend of events called Canaltown Days; for a schedule write to Historic Palmyra, Inc., P.O. Box 96, Palmyra 14522, or call the village offices at 315-597-6700.

A mile and a half down Church Street is a cobblestone house on the Martin Harris Farm. Harris was intrigued by Joseph Smith's translation of the Book of Mormon; eventually he mortgaged his farm to pay for its first printing. Harris's wife remained skeptical, however, and she purloined 116 pages of Smith's translation. This section was never retranslated. The unbelieving Mrs. Harris moved to her half of the farm, and Martin Harris eventually lost his.

The handsome cobblestone house postdates Harris's ownership, though the well in front of it is believed to have been dug by Joseph Smith's father and brother. Inside, the house is modern, with displays telling Harris's story.

Past the Harris farm, the railroad tracks at the bottom of the hill are rather bumpy.

8.1 Soon after Center Road enters from the left, turn right onto Jeffrey Road.

MARK ROTH

Joseph Smith's house is one of the sites near Palmyra associated with the founding of the Mormon Church.

Here you begin riding up and down the steep east and west sides of drumlins.

9.5 At the stop sign, turn left onto NY 21 North.

10.4 Turn right onto Goldsmith Road.

11.2 Keep right at the fork, which brings you up to Shilling (sometimes spelled Schilling) Road, heading south.

11.4 Turn left onto Lusk Road.

12.1 At the T-junction, turn right onto Harris Road.

12.7 Turn left at the stop sign onto North Creek Road, CR 223.

13.6 Follow the road to the left, uphill, after passing a turnoff to Whitbeck Road. At the top of the hill, continue straight; do not take Lyon Road. (You will see a cobblestone building on your left.)

14.0 Turn right at the stop sign onto Hydesville Road, CR 221.
Just less than 3 miles farther, at Parker Road, on the left is a site associated with

one of the quasi-religious movements of the 19th century, which earned the area the sobriquet "burned-over district." Here lived the Fox sisters, founders of modern spiritualism. The "Hydesville rappings" began in 1848 when two of the Fox girls, Margaret and Catherine, reported strange knocking. The teenage girls soon invented a code to communicate with the source of the sounds, claiming that it was the uneasy spirit of a peddler murdered in the house some years before. There were skeptics, but also a surprising number of believers. Soon the girls were holding séances in nearby Rochester. With an older sister as publicist and booking agent, the Fox sisters were soon among the most famous people in pre–Civil War America. Séances were held for U.S. senators and such notables as Horace Greeley, James Fenimore Cooper, William Cullen Bryant, George Ripley, and the wife of President Franklin Pierce.

After decades of travel, fame and infamy, adulation and scorn, wealth and scrimping, Margaret Fox admitted that the early Hydesville rappings had been produced with an apple on a string. Later the girls learned to make a suitable sound by cracking a joint in the foot, which made their act portable. In 1888, in a speech at the Academy of Music in Brooklyn, New York, Margaret Fox apologized for the "horrible deception." Despite that, the Fox sisters' brand of spiritualism has adherents today.

17.7 Turn right at the stop sign onto NY 88 South.
In just less than a mile and a half, Newark Canal County Park to the left borders the Barge Canal and has a picnic area.

19.5 After passing the center of Newark, turn right onto High Street, opposite a small park with a statue in the middle.

19.7 Turn left at the stop sign onto Mason Street.
On the right at this intersection is the Newark Public Library, which houses the Hoffman Clock Museum. Its antique timepieces can be seen during library hours. Admission is free.

19.8 At the stop sign, turn right onto West Maple Avenue.

20.4 Turn left at the stop sign onto Peirson Avenue.

21.1 Turn right onto Pardy Smith Road.

22.5 At the T-junction, turn right onto Turner Road, and, in 150 yards, turn left onto Short Road.

23.5 At the T-junction, make a left turn onto Field Street, and then make a quick right onto Wilber Road.

24.3 Turn left at the T-junction onto CR 7.

24.5 Pass the intersection with CR 27, and 100 yards farther turn right onto Armington School Road.

27.5 Turn left onto NY 21 South. In a little more than a mile you'll be back at Hill Cumorah. (If you have energy left, the paved road to the top of the hill is 0.6 mile long.)

Nearby Bed-and-Breakfasts

Canaltown B&B, 119 Canandaigua Street, Palmyra (315-597-5553)

Bicycle Shops

Geneva Bicycle Center, 489 Exchange Street, Geneva (315-789-5922)

Snow Country Bike Shop, Parkway Plaza, NY 5 and US 20, Canandaigua (585-394-1530)

–Updated by Rob Clark

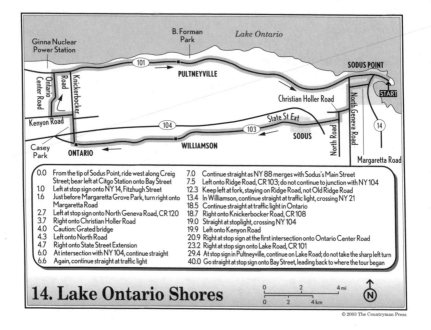

Ginna Nuclear
Power Station

B. Forman
Park

Lake Ontario

101

PULTNEYVILLE

SODUS POINT

START

Ontario
Center Road

Knickerbocker
Road

Christian Holler Road

North Geneva Road

14

Kenyon Road

104

State St Ext

103

SODUS

North Road

Casey
Park

ONTARIO

WILLIAMSON

Margaretta Road

Mile	Directions	Mile	Directions
0.0	From the tip of Sodus Point, ride west along Creig Street; bear left at Citgo Station onto Bay Street	7.0	Continue straight as NY 88 merges with Sodus's Main Street
1.0	Left at stop sign onto NY 14, Fitzhugh Street	7.5	Left onto Ridge Road, CR 103; do not continue to junction with NY 104
1.6	Just before Margaretta Grove Park, turn right onto Margaretta Road	12.3	Keep left at fork, staying on Ridge Road, not Old Ridge Road
2.7	Left at stop sign onto North Geneva Road, CR 120	13.4	In Williamson, continue straight at traffic light, crossing NY 21
3.7	Right onto Christian Holler Road	18.5	Continue straight at traffic light in Ontario
4.0	Caution: Grated bridge	18.7	Right onto Knickerbocker Road, CR 108
4.3	Left onto North Road	19.0	Straight at stoplight, crossing NY 104
4.7	Right onto State Street Extension	19.9	Left onto Kenyon Road
6.0	At intersection with NY 104, continue straight	20.9	Right at stop sign at the first intersection onto Ontario Center Road
6.6	Again, continue straight at traffic light	23.2	Right at stop sign onto Lake Road, CR 101
		29.4	At stop sign in Pultneyville, continue on Lake Road; do not take the sharp left turn
		40.0	Go straight at stop sign onto Bay Street, leading back to where the tour began

14. Lake Ontario Shores

0   2   4 mi
0   2   4 km

N

Lake Ontario Shores

- **DISTANCE:** 40 miles; easy cycling
- **TERRAIN:** Mostly level terrain with some low hills
- **COUNTY MAP:** Wayne

This Wayne County route takes the cyclist along roads bordered by orchards, orchards, and more orchards. From mid-May flowering to autumn maturity, a scene of bucolic order pleases the eye as rows of carefully tended fruit trees pattern lowlands and gentle rises. It will come as no surprise that Wayne County ranks first in the state in apple production and is fourth in sour cherries; peaches, plums, apricots, and pears complete the countywide fruit salad.

The fruit orchards are here because of Lake Ontario's moderating influence on the weather; the lake is also indirectly responsible for the large number of cobblestone houses. This masonry is unique to the region south of the lake, cobbles having been formed in former lake beds and along earlier shorelines. The first cobblestone houses were built in the area sometime around 1825, probably by masons who had worked on the Erie Canal locks. A high quality of craftsmanship, and care in selection of stones depending on size, shape, and color, produced many houses of distinction. The Lake Ontario lowland and northern Finger Lakes areas have some 800 cobblestone houses extant; Wayne County leads all others with about 175. More than 20 such buildings are seen along this route.

The lake makes one more contribution to the appeal of this tour: Both Ridge Road and Lake Road, one following a former and the other the present shoreline, provide miles of level cycling; a major east–west highway running between the two draws off most of the through traffic. There are opportunities for swimming and fishing on this excursion as well as several attractive B&Bs near Sodus Point.

Begin the ride at the tip of Sodus Point, on the west side of Sodus Bay. Please park your car at the municipal parking lot next to the hot dog stand. The starting point is in a residential area at the tip of the peninsula, so it is best to leave your car in the commercial section of the village and cycle to the starting point at the end of the peninsula.

0.0 From the tip of Sodus Point you can ride in only one direction, west, along Creig Street. Bear left at the Citgo Station onto Bay Street.

The spit of land that forms Creig and Bay Streets, along with other bars and islands, gives Sodus Bay outstanding natural protection from Lake Ontario storms. Capt. Charles Williamson, in charge of developing much of western New York for the English Pulteney interests during the last decade of the 18th century, considered it "the best harbour on the south side of Lake Ontario. Few or none, even on the seacoast, exceed it for spaciousness and beauty."

Though it flourished briefly, the town on the bay did not live up to the expectations of early speculators. Burned to the ground by the British during the War of 1812, it suffered further setbacks as a port after the completion of the Erie Canal in 1825.

Also in the 19th century, railroad tycoon Edward H. Harriman had grandiose plans for development; little remains of these designs except Margaretta Grove, a small park given to the town by Mrs. Harriman, which you'll pass on your way out of the village.

Today Sodus Point is largely a summer playground for fishing and boating; sailing is particularly popular in the sheltered waters. Along the north shore of the town, Sodus Point Park has picnic facilities and a bathhouse for swimmers. There are several small restaurants and grocery stores along Bay Street. Similar-size businesses appear in most of the villages along the route, with one large restaurant near the end of the tour.

A right turn onto Ontario Street (the last house on the right before this turn

*once belonged to the Harrimans) leads toward the lake and Big Sodus Light,
restored and maintained by the Sodus Bay Historical Society. The first lighthouse
on this site was built in 1825 and was replaced by the present structure in 1871.
The lighthouse-museum is open Saturday and Sunday 1–5 PM. South of the lighthouse, what had once been the installation's carriage house has been adapted for
use as guest rooms by the Carriage House Inn.*

1.0 Turn left at the stop sign onto NY 14, Fitzhugh Street.

1.6 Just before Margaretta Grove Park, turn right onto Margaretta Road.

2.7 Turn left at the stop sign, onto North Geneva Road, CR 120.

3.7 Turn right onto Christian Holler Road.
*The road's unusual name is said to come from an odd, and presumably noisy, sect
of Christian fatalists who predicted the world would end in 1823.*

4.0 Caution: Grated bridge.

4.3 Turn left onto North Road.

4.7 Turn right onto State Street Extension.
*The orchards that you have begun riding through will continue with few interrup-
tions until you are back at Sodus Point. One reason for good fruit production is
that Lake Ontario retards the season a bit, providing a cool spring and some protection from early autumn frosts; thus buds are less likely to be nipped by a May
freeze, and fruit can be harvested into October.*

6.0 At the intersection with NY 104, continue straight.

6.6 Again, continue straight at the traffic light.
*Sodus has long been the site of fruit-processing plants, and in the 1880s it led the
nation in apple drying. Sodus earlier made attempts to start a silk business, which
an 1838 newspaper declared was "as simple as feeding pigs and very easy to per-
form, one in which small children could be made useful, and also decayed widows
and decrepit females. . . ." But the mulberry trees did not thrive and the industry
died.*

*A major fire gutted downtown Sodus after the turn of the 20th century; the
rebuilding was not very successful, and the town does not reflect the bountiful
aspect of its countryside.*

7.0 Continue straight as NY 88 merges with Sodus's Main Street.

MARK ROTH

Cobblestone construction is indigenous to the northern Finger Lakes–Lake Ontario lowlands area.

7.5 Turn left onto Ridge Road, CR 103; do not continue to the junction with NY 104.

Ridge Road follows a low rise marking a former shoreline of a larger precursor to Lake Ontario, which geologists call glacial Lake Iroquois. As you ride, the land to your right was once lake bottom. The ridge served as a natural highway for soldiers and early settlers, and later it supported a Rochester–Sodus Point trolley with spring excursions advertised as "forty miles of blossoms." The ridge was also an easily accessible source of fine, water-smoothed cobblestones for house construction.

Cobblestone construction started as a simple, cheap expedient for farm buildings, but it quickly became popular with people who could afford to build with other materials. Though all cobblestones result from glacial action, they are divided into two types—ice-laid, or field cobbles, and water-laid, if they received a final tumbling and smoothing in stream or lake after being released from the ice. Water-laid cobbles are smaller, smoother, and rounder than field cobbles; they were suited for delicate designs or patterns and were often used for the fronts of houses, while field cobbles were relegated to side and rear sections. Since cobblestone construction peaked in the 1830s and '40s, most houses are in the Greek Revival style then popular, though a few Gothic Revival or Italianate homes survive. You'll count nearly two dozen cobblestone structures along this route; many are on the ridge itself.

12.3 Keep left at the fork, staying on Ridge Road, not Old Ridge Road.
In this area you may notice a derelict windmill and many Dutch names on mailboxes. East Williamson is still predominantly Dutch, populated by descendants of settlers who arrived between 1840 and 1845.

13.4 In the village of Williamson, continue straight at the traffic light, crossing NY 21.
Williamson considers itself the fruit capital of the county and annually celebrates Apple Blossom Time, a weeklong festival in mid-May. Cycle at that time of year and you'll pedal among a profusion of blossoms.

Just outside of Williamson, there's a cobblestone building converted for use as a gas station. It is only in the last few decades that cobblestone structures have been treated as historic landmarks, and some still serve mundane purposes.

18.5 Continue straight at the traffic light in the village of Ontario.
Ontario has small luncheonettes and a natural foods grocery.

18.7 Turn right onto Knickerbocker Road, CR 108.

19.0 Go straight at the stoplight, crossing NY 104.
A little more than half a mile farther is the entrance to Casey Park, which occupies the site of a former surface iron ore mine. A Mr. Knickerbocker discovered the ore deposit in 1811, and mining and smelting were important local industries in the 19th century. Activity peaked in the 1880s, and then declined rapidly after the discovery of the rich Mesabi Range in Minnesota. Small workings to supply dye to makers of red barn paint continued through the 1940s. A mile-long excavation is filled with spring water and makes a fine swimming site. The bordering parallel ridges are mine tailings. A map in the park points out other area landmarks connected with the mine.

19.9 Turn left onto Kenyon Road.

20.9 Turn right at the stop sign at the first intersection onto Ontario Center Road.
A mile farther, at the Brick Church Road crossing, is Heritage Square, which

preserves a log cabin and a one-room school. May through September it is open weekends, 1:30–5 PM, although the working pump can be used to fill water bottles at any time.

23.2 At the stop sign, turn right onto Lake Road, CR 101.
Across the road, behind the innocuous Ginna training center sign, is the Ginna Nuclear Power Station of Rochester Gas and Electric. Ginna made headlines in January 1982 when it vented radioactivity into the atmosphere.

You'll have your first good view of Lake Ontario shortly, with opportunities for fishing at the boat-launching sites.

29.4 At the stop sign in Pultneyville, continue on Lake Road as it turns about 30 degrees to the left. Do not take the sharp left turn; follow Seaway Trail instead.
Pultneyville is finely preserved, with grand old houses fortunate to have owners with the will and ability to keep them up. Rochester journalist Arch Merrill is not guilty of much hyperbole in writing, "Pultneyville is a dream village, a bit of old New England's shore—without the stern and rock-bound coast—and in a fairer, greener land." Pultneyville was a thriving village of ships' captains, many from New England, who preferred to live in sight of water in houses of familiar style. By the time lake shipping and ocean whaling declined, rich Rochester people were ready to take the captains' houses for summer or year-round residences.

A monument by the shore recalls the captains and ships of Pultneyville's booming years of sail. Another recounts the defense of the town against British forces during the War of 1812. Local men did gather hastily under General Swift on May 15, 1814; the plaque omits to mention that they surrendered the next day.

Less than a mile past Pultneyville is B. Forman Park, with picnic tables, rest rooms, and drinking water. This originated as Camp Forman, a recreation area for employees of the Rochester-based apparel firm.

About 4 miles farther, Cinelli's Country House Restaurant sits amid meticulous lawns overlooking acres of orchards. An anomaly in this rural fruit land, Cinelli's draws distant urbanites to sample the homemade Italian specialties. The restaurant serves Tuesday through Friday noon–2 PM and 5–9 PM, Saturday 5–10 PM, and Sunday 1–8 PM.

40.0 Go straight at the stop sign onto Bay Street, leading back to where the tour began at Sodus Bay, which Williamson, ever the promoter, proclaimed "one of the most magnificent landscapes the human fancy can picture."

Nearby Bed-and-Breakfasts

Carriage House Inn, 8375 Wickham Boulevard, Sodus Point (315-483-2100)

Silver Waters Guest House, 8420 Bay Street, Sodus Point (315-483-8098)

Bicycle Shops

Snow Country Bike Shop, Parkway Plaza, NY 5 and US 20, Canandaigua (585-394-1530)

—Updated by John and Cathy Van Vechten

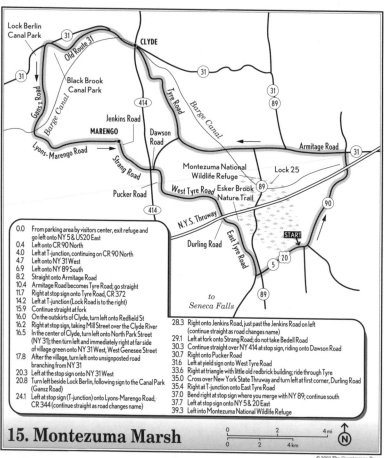

Lock Berlin Canal Park

CLYDE

Old Route 31

Black Brook Canal Park

Gansz Road

Barge Canal

Jenkins Road

MARENGO

Lyons-Marengo Road

414

Tyre Road

Barge Canal

Dawson Road

Strang Road

Montezuma National Wildlife Refuge

Lock 25

Armitage Road

31

31
89

31

Pucker Road

West Tyre Road

Esker Brook Nature Trail

89

414

N.Y.S. Thruway

90

Durling Road

East Tyre Road

START

to Seneca Falls

5
20

89

0.0	From parking area at visitors center, exit refuge and go left onto NY 5 & US20 East
0.4	Left onto CR 90 North
4.0	Left at T-junction, continuing on CR 90 North
4.7	Left onto NY 31 West
6.9	Left onto NY 89 South
8.2	Straight onto Armitage Road
10.4	Armitage Road becomes Tyre Road; go straight
11.7	Right at stop sign onto Tyre Road, CR 372
14.2	Left at T-junction (Lock Road is to the right)
15.9	Continue straight at fork
16.0	On the outskirts of Clyde, turn left onto Redfield St
16.2	Right at stop sign, taking Mill Street over the Clyde River
16.5	In the center of Clyde, turn left onto North Park Street (NY 31); then turn left and immediately right at far side of village green onto NY 31 West, West Genesee Street
17.8	After the village, turn left onto unsignposted road branching from NY 31
20.3	Left at the stop sign onto NY 31 West
20.8	Turn left beside Lock Berlin, following sign to the Canal Park (Gansz Road)
24.1	Left at stop sign (T-junction) onto Lyons-Marengo Road, CR 344 (continue straight as road changes name)

28.3	Right onto Jenkins Road, just past the Jenkins Road on left (continue straight as road changes name)
29.1	Left at fork onto Strang Road; do not take Bedell Road
30.3	Continue straight over NY 414 at stop sign, riding onto Dawson Road
30.7	Right onto Pucker Road
31.6	Left at yield sign onto West Tyre Road
33.6	Right at triangle with little old redbrick building; ride through Tyre
35.0	Cross over New York State Thruway and turn left at first corner, Durling Road
35.4	Right at T-junction onto East Tyre Road
37.0	Bend right at stop sign where you merge with NY 89; continue south
37.7	Left at stop sign onto NY 5 & 20 East
39.3	Left into Montezuma National Wildlife Refuge

15. Montezuma Marsh

0   2   4 mi

0   2   4 km

N

© 2003 The Countryman Press

Montezuma Marsh

- **DISTANCE:** 39 miles; easy to moderate cycling
- **TERRAIN:** Many low hills and some level stretches
- **COUNTY MAPS:** Seneca, Wayne

Few people ever said the Montezuma Marsh was beautiful. Except for itinerant outlaws, it had few human inhabitants with the means to get away. It bred mosquitoes and other noisome bugs; it exuded what in the 19th century was believed to be "bad air," known now as malaria; it mired wagons; it was not good for corn, wheat, or cattle; and it made construction of the Erie Canal almost impossible.

But if you could get the opinion of birds—especially of geese and ducks—you'd get another picture altogether. A fine place, they might say, with water to swim in, weeds to eat, muck and quicksand to discourage predators. Human perceptions differing so radically from avian ones, it is understandable that the Montezuma Marsh was almost drained dry in the early years of the 20th century, and that it did not become a National Wildlife Refuge until 1938. Since then, bird and bird-fancier have delighted in Montezuma, especially during spring and fall migration seasons. As this tour begins at Montezuma, an early start can get you there while the mist is rising and the geese, herons, coots, muskrats, and deer are breakfasting placidly. The 4-mile-long gravel road through the refuge is well graded and little used.

MARK ROTH

The double locks at Lock Berlin Canal Park are the best set surviving from the old Erie Canal.

You'll border or cross several waterways along this route, some natural, some man-made. Though the old Erie Canal, completed in 1825, is virtually gone, you can explore its best-preserved relics at the Lock Berlin Canal Park. The 1918 Barge Canal uses sections of the old Erie and parts of natural rivers and lakes. (The Erie had to be wholly man-made in order to control the water level through flood and drought.) The Barge Canal today caters mostly to pleasure craft, and you pass an operating lock along this route. East of Montezuma Marsh you'll see the Cayuga and Seneca Canal, linking the two longest Finger Lakes to the Barge Canal system.

There are no concessions in or near the refuge, so you may want to bring food with you. The village of Clyde, about a third of the way through the route, has a grocery store and a couple of restaurants.

The tour starts in the parking area of the Montezuma National Wildlife Refuge, off NY 5 and US 20, 3 miles east of Seneca Falls.

The refuge no longer allows walkers or cyclists to go through. We suggest you enjoy the refuge in your car, before or after your ride. It is open during daylight hours, road conditions allowing.

0.0 From the parking area by the visitors center, exit the refuge and take a left onto NY 5 and US 20 East.

At the visitors center are displays of stuffed birds, maps, and useful explanatory pamphlets. There is also a clipboard for recording recent bird sightings, and details on refuge areas temporarily closed to visitors. To see birds and other wildlife, it is best to start as soon after dawn as possible, ideally on a weekday.

Montezuma National Wildlife Refuge's approximately 10 square miles of wetland and field are visited by thousands of waterfowl traveling the Atlantic Flyway. In April and October, migrating geese and ducks number about 150,000. Little can compare to the thrill of seeing—and hearing—thousands of Canada geese leaving the refuge in the morning or returning at dusk. At peak times you can see phalanxes of geese in every quadrant of the sky. Warblers are common in May and June, and many other birds and mammals, including deer, are seen throughout the year. Since 1976 a program to reestablish bald eagles in New York has used Montezuma as a hacking site, so it is possible to see one of these extremely rare birds flying free. Warm-water fish, particularly the bullhead, northern pike, and walleye, draw anglers to the waters bordering the refuge.

Before the swamp was drained in 1911, Montezuma Marsh was 12 miles long and 8 miles wide, one of the largest freshwater marshes in North America. With contiguous Cayuga Lake it was a formidable barrier to east–west travel. In The Erie Canal, *Ralph Andrist recounts that for diggers of the canal, relief at the easy shoveling was short-lived: Cuttings oozed full of mud, quicksand swallowed retaining walls, leeches and mosquitoes attacked; in 1819 more than one thousand men died of malaria at Montezuma. A harried doctor by chance tried a new drug from Peru, which happened to contain quinine. The canal was dug; but not before the men had added a new verse to their ballad of woes:*

We are digging the Ditch through the mire;
Through the mud and the slime and the mire, by heck!
And the mud is our principal hire;
In our pants, up our sleeves, down our neck, by heck!
The mud is our principal hire.

0.4 Turn left onto CR 90 North.

4.0 Turn left at the T-junction, continuing on CR 90 North.

4.7 Turn left onto NY 31 West.

6.9 Turn left onto NY 89 South.

8.2 Go straight onto Armitage Road. At this intersection Wayne County begins and NY 89 turns right.
Beside Armitage Road, lowlands are diked and drained by gravity and pumps so that potatoes and celery can be raised on the rich, heavy muckland soil. You will ride over two one-lane bridges.

10.4 At the Galen town line, Armitage Road becomes Tyre Road. Go straight here (gravel road is to your left).

11.7 At the stop sign, turn right on Tyre Road, CR 372.

14.2 Turn left at the T-junction (Lock Road is to the right of the T-junction).

15.9 Continue straight at the fork.

16.0 On the outskirts of Clyde, turn left onto Redfield Street.

16.2 Turn right at the stop sign, taking Mill Street over the Clyde River.
Here the river carries Barge Canal traffic; the old Erie ran a few rods south of the river.

16.5 In the center of the village of Clyde, turn left onto North Park Street (NY 31). At the far side of the village green, turn left and immediately right to follow NY 31 West, West Genesee Street.
Clyde was named for the Scottish river in 1818, and its main thoroughfare is Glasgow Street; yet this canal town has had a large Italian community since the 1860s, when immigrant labor was needed for railroad construction and later for widening the Erie Canal. The statue of George Washington on the village green was erected during World War II by the Sons of Italy to allay suspicions about their allegiance.
   A pioneer glass factory, in operation here until 1912, developed the Mason-type fruit jar.

17.8 After you've left the village, turn left onto the unsignposted road branching from NY 31.
This narrow road, rough in parts, is Old Route 31. A relic from the days of smaller and slower cars, it gets little traffic.

Two and a third miles farther is Black Brook Canal Park, with picnic tables and a covered shelter, rest rooms, and drinking water. A path from the right side of the picnic shelter leads, in about 100 feet, to the original Erie Canal, where a grassy track follows the old towpath. Canal buffs may want to walk the 0.8 mile to Lock Berlin to rejoin the cycling route there. If so, walk west on the towpath.

20.3 Turn left at the stop sign onto NY 31 West.

20.8 Turn left beside the hamlet of Lock Berlin, following a sign to the Canal Park (Gansz Road). You will see a one-lane bridge 100 yards down the road. Lock Berlin Canal Park has picnic tables, rest rooms, and cold well water. But the real attraction is the finest set of locks remaining from the Erie Canal. If the gate is unlocked, a small bridge allows you to reach an artificial island between the locks to examine every scratch and rope-worn stone in detail.

Legend and folklore have embellished the romance of the old canal, yet exaggerating its importance would be difficult. Before it was built, the longest canal in America was the 27-mile-long Middlesex Canal in Massachusetts; the Erie was to cross 363 miles of wilderness and need 83 locks. Even the perspicacious Thomas Jefferson, while admitting the canal was a good idea, declared that it was a century too soon, and "little short of madness to think of at this day." For once, Jefferson was wrong; in 1817 New York State forged ahead. In October 1825, the Erie was completed. The Midwest was opened to rapid settlement, farmers gained access to distant markets, and cities from Buffalo to New York sprang up like mushrooms and prospered.

Lock Berlin was number 27 on the Erie Canal. It is made of Medina limestone, smooth except where it was hammered to give better footing. Coping stones are worn at their edges by tow ropes. When open, gates swung into recesses in side walls for ease of passage. These heavy gates could be opened by one man aided by the leverage from a long balance beam that pivoted on a post set in the semicircular end of the gate recess. The splayed grooves you can see near the post secured metal bracing and were not tracks for moving parts. A small sluice gate operated by a separate control meant that the large lock gate never had to be pushed against water at a different level.

Past the Canal Park you ride under a railroad tunnel, then up the typically steep north-facing slope of a drumlin. The orchards around you are just a small sample of Wayne County's abundant fruit production; in acres planted, the county leads the state in apples, cherries, and pears. (For a daylong ride through Wayne County orchards, see Tour 14.)

24.1 Turn left at the stop sign (T-junction) onto Lyons-Marengo Road, CR 344. After crossing the bridge over the Barge Canal and Clyde River, stay on Lyons-Marengo Road. Keep to the road you are riding, though it changes name—first becoming Clyde-Marengo Road and then Turnpike Road (continue straight here).
The hamlet of Marengo was once a bustling stagecoach stop on the Montezuma Turnpike, an early privately owned toll road made unprofitable by the Erie Canal.

28.3 Turn right onto Jenkins Road, just past the Jenkins Road on your left.
Keep going straight at the Seneca County line, where the name changes to Strang Road.

29.1 At the fork, keep left on Strang Road; do not take Bedell Road.

30.3 Continue straight over NY 414 at the stop sign, riding onto Dawson Road.

30.7 Turn right onto Pucker Road.

31.6 At the yield sign, turn left onto West Tyre Road.

33.6 At the triangle with a little old redbrick building, turn right. Ride through the village of Tyre and climb the short hill, keeping the church on your immediate right.

35.0 After crossing over the New York State Thruway, turn left at the first corner, Durling Road.

35.4 Turn right at the T-junction onto East Tyre Road.
In 0.3 mile you'll arrive at a small parking area giving access to the Esker Brook Nature Trail of the Montezuma National Wildlife Refuge. The trail is about two miles long.

37.0 At the stop sign where you merge with NY 89, bend to the right so that you continue south.

37.7 Turn left at the stop sign onto NY 5 and US 20 East.

39.3 Turn left into the Montezuma National Wildlife Refuge.
Your starting point may look the same as when you left, or bird activity hours later may be markedly different.

Bicycle Shops

Bicycles Today, 360 Grant Avenue, Auburn (315-253-0585)

Geneva Bicycle Center, 493 Exchange Street, Geneva (315-789-5922)

M & R Sports, 286 Clark Street, Auburn (315-252-9069)

Nolan's Sporting Goods, 41 Genesee Street, Auburn (315-252-7249)

—Updated by Michael Priestman

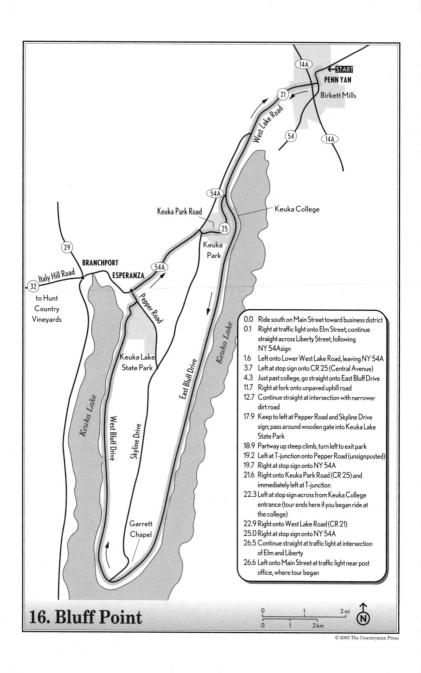

0.0   Ride south on Main Street toward business district
0.1   Right at traffic light onto Elm Street; continue straight across Liberty Street, following NY 54A sign
1.6   Left onto Lower West Lake Road, leaving NY 54A
3.7   Left at stop sign onto CR 25 (Central Avenue)
4.3   Just past college, go straight onto East Bluff Drive
11.7 Right at fork onto unpaved uphill road
12.7 Continue straight at intersection with narrower dirt road
17.9 Keep to left at Pepper Road and Skyline Drive sign; pass around wooden gate into Keuka Lake State Park
18.9 Partway up steep climb, turn left to exit park
19.2 Left at T-junction onto Pepper Road (unsignposted)
19.7 Right at stop sign onto NY 54A
21.6 Right onto Keuka Park Road (CR 25) and immediately left at T-junction
22.3 Left at stop sign across from Keuka College entrance (tour ends here if you began ride at the college)
22.9 Right onto West Lake Road (CR 21)
25.0 Right at stop sign onto NY 54A
26.5 Continue straight at traffic light at intersection of Elm and Liberty
26.6 Left onto Main Street at traffic light near post office, where tour began

16. Bluff Point

0   1   2 mi
0   1   2 km

N

© 2003 The Countryman Press

Bluff Point

- **DISTANCE:** 27 or 19 miles; mostly easy, with some moderate cycling
- **TERRAIN:** Level to slightly undulating, with one long climb
- **COUNTY MAP:** Yates

The prospects over Keuka Lake from many points surrounding its 60-mile shoreline are some of the very finest in the entire region. Keuka, formerly known as Crooked Lake, is the only one of the Finger Lakes shaped like a Y; its two north branches are separated by a high, rounded peninsula, known as the bluff, fringed with forests and crowned by vineyards. The road along the peninsula's shore circles back to within a couple of miles of its starting point; as a result it is used only by local residents and a few sightseers. About 1.5 miles are unpaved. Following the waterside, tree-shaded bluff road, you'll enjoy the longest stretch of quiet lakeside riding found in any of these tours, and you'll take in exquisite views of this multifingered waterway from elevations accessible with a minimum of hill-climbing. You'll have the opportunity to fish or swim at beautifully situated Keuka Lake State Park. A diversion of 4 miles allows for a winery visit. In late September you can attend Penn Yan's Buckwheat Festival, with various entertainment, cooking demonstrations, and pancake dinners.

Directions are given from the village of Penn Yan, but those who want to bicycle less and swim, fish, or wine-taste more can cut almost 8 miles by driving to Keuka College in Keuka Park and starting the tour there. Fast riders, or those spending another day in the area, may also enjoy riding the 7.5 miles of Skyline Drive along the crest of the bluff.

Start the tour in front of the post office on Main Street in Penn Yan, located at the north end of Keuka Lake's east branch.

0.0 Ride south on Main Street, toward the business district.

The town's peculiar name resulted from an 1810 compromise between rival groups of settlers—Pennsylvanians and New England Yankees. This was some years after the Wagener family established the first homestead. It was on their farm that the first Wagener apple was developed, and Wagener Street, just south of the starting point of this ride, runs through their former orchard. Birkett Mills, the largest producer of buckwheat products in the country, occupies the site of one of Wagener's first gristmills, where Main Street crosses the Keuka Lake outlet. Visitors can purchase Birkett products at its modern Main Street office next to the post office.

There are many restaurants in and around Penn Yan, and several grocery stores. There are no other sources for food on this tour after leaving the village, so you should carry what you need with you.

0.1 Turn right at the traffic light onto Elm Street; continue straight across Liberty Street, following the sign for NY 54A.

In about a mile the Seneca Farms ice cream store on the left provides covered picnic tables for patrons, plus excellent ice cream. Next to Seneca Farms, Ritchey Road leads down to Indian Pines Park, with swimming and picnicking facilities.

At 351 Elm Street, the Wagener Estate Bed & Breakfast occupies the historic building that was once home to two of the area's earliest settlers, David and Rebecca Wagener, in the 1790s. Rates start at $99 for a double (315-536-4591).

1.6 Turn left onto Lower West Lake Road, leaving NY 54A.

You may have noticed a sign for Jerusalem township. The name is from the settlement established by followers of Jemima Wilkinson, who came to the wilderness area east and north of Keuka Lake to set up a "New Jerusalem." Penn Yan pioneer David Wagener, formerly of Pennsylvania, was one of these "Jemimakins." Wilkinson claimed that she had died and had come back as the androgynous "Publick Universal Friend," opposed to marriage and to private property other than her own. Although her sermons were said to have been almost unintelligible, "with sufficient verbosity, with a confused mass of scriptural quotations, and almost always with obscurity, which sometimes was impenetrable," she steadily gathered

The Garrett Memorial Chapel commands a wide view over Keuka Lake.

converts from her native New England and Pennsylvania. As her detractors increased proportionately, she gave up her original plan of converting the entire world and sent some of the sect's members in search of a wilderness retreat in the newly opened Finger Lakes area.

After they made their initial settlement in the present town of Milo on the west shore of Seneca Lake in 1788, dissension among the Jemimakins resulted in the removal of a portion of the group, along with the Friend herself, to the area now called Jerusalem. There a house was erected for her in 1815; today it is a private residence on Friend Hill Road, about 6 miles west of Penn Yan.

Defections and the obvious limits to the growth of a sect believing in celibacy reduced the settlement's population; when the Friend "left time" for good in 1819, the sect disintegrated.

3.7 Turn left at the stop sign onto CR 25, also known as Central Avenue.
In about a half mile you'll see the main entrance to the Keuka College campus on your left. (Begin the tour here if you want to shorten it by about 8 miles.) Ball Hall (1889), opposite the entrance, dates from the founding of this four-year women's college; most of the other buildings are modern. The 173-acre campus has more than a half mile of beachfront and is the site of the annual mid-August Keuka Arts Festival. The Dahlstrom Student Center has a cafeteria and bookstore open only during the academic year, but rest rooms and drinking water are available throughout the summer.

4.3 Just past the college, go straight onto East Bluff Drive.
Because this road becomes unpaved when it reaches the tip of the bluff, there is little through traffic. To your left the east branch of the lake is lined with neat cottages, while on your right the bluff rises steeply some 700 feet. Chipmunks and woodchucks sun themselves next to the quiet roadway, and your chances of glimpsing deer on the wooded bluffside are good.

11.7 At the fork, turn right onto the unpaved uphill road. (East Bluff Road Extension becomes unpaved and virtually impassable in a mile or so.)
The uphill climb lasts for 0.6 mile, and shortly thereafter you are rewarded with a view of the meeting of the east and west branches of Keuka Lake, and the single trunk extending to the south. The shape resulted from glacial deepening of valleys made by south-flowing streams. The branched lake is now unique in the Finger Lakes. All the Finger Lakes empty to the north, Keuka being again unique in having two inlets, at its northwestern and southern tips, with an outlet to the north-

east. Thus, water entering from the northwest drifts south, rounds the bluff, and flows north to the outlet at Penn Yan.

12.7 Continue straight at the intersection with a narrower dirt road.
The exceptional view from Bluff Point has long been appreciated. Charles Williamson, pioneer land agent of the Finger Lakes, chose this as a site for one of his homes, and Abraham Wagener, son of Penn Yan's first settler, built the still surviving Wagener Manor House here in the 1830s. More recently it became the site of a chapel built in 1931 by wine magnate Paul Garrett and his wife, in memory of their son, Charles, who died of tuberculosis at the age of 28. Services are held here at 11 AM every Sunday in the summer. The chapel is also open Wednesday afternoon 1–4 PM. To visit the isolated granite memorial and its forested chapel yard, turn right onto the narrow dirt road at the tip of the bluff. You'll reach the chapel after a stiff 0.5-mile climb.

The mile and a half of unpaved road makes a half circle around the tip of the bluff and now goes north, becoming West Bluff Drive. The view from the bluff justifies naturalist Samuel Hammond's 1854 proclamation that "there is no more beautiful sheet of water anywhere else in the world than Keuka."

17.9 At the bottom of a long hill, a sign to the right indicates the way to Pepper Road and Skyline Drive. Keep to the left here, passing around a wooden gate (with no parking and fire and ambulance signs) into Keuka Lake State Park.
This 621-acre state park provides facilities for swimming, picnicking, fishing, and boating. There are 150 campsites available mid-May to mid-October. Swimming is excellent in Keuka Lake, and many campers bring boats to launch. There are also hiking and bridle trails.

18.9 Partway up a steep climb, turn left to exit the park.

19.2 At the T-junction, turn left onto Pepper Road (unsignposted).

19.7 Turn right at the stop sign onto NY 54A.
High on a hill across the road at this junction is an imposing stucco Greek Revival mansion, started in 1823 and completed in 1838. For many years it served as the county poorhouse; in 1979 it became a winery, which operated until 1986.

Those willing to tackle a steep downhill and uphill each way can visit a winery by turning left here instead of right and riding down the hill to the village of Branchport. Continue straight through town and head up Italy Hill Road. In about a mile you'll come to the Hunt Country Vineyards, operated by descendants of Aaron Hunt, who *purchased the land in the early 19th century. Open Monday through Saturday 10–5 PM, and Sunday 12-5 PM this winery offers a half-hour haywagon tour of its vineyards, charging $1.50 for those older than 10. The wine shop offers free wine samples. Retrace the 2 miles to Pepper Road to rejoin the tour.*

21.6 Turn right onto Keuka Park Road (CR 25) and immediately left at the T-junction.

22.3 Turn left at the stop sign across from the entrance to Keuka College. (If you elected to begin at the college, the tour ends here.)

22.9 Turn right onto West Lake Road (CR 21).

25.0 Turn right at the stop sign onto NY 54A.

26.5 Continue straight at the traffic light at the intersection of Elm and Liberty.

26.6 Turn left onto Main Street at the traffic light near the post office, where the tour began.
A little farther north and on the left at 200 Main Street is the Oliver House. Built in 1852 and used as a home by three generations of doctors, it now houses the Yates County Historical Society. Some personal belongings of Jemima Wilkinson are preserved here, plus other items of local history. The house is open 9 AM–5 PM Monday through Friday.

Nearby Bed-and-Breakfasts

Finton's Landing, 661 East Lake Road, Penn Yan (315-536-3146)

The Fox Inn, 158 Main Street, Penn Yan (315-536-3101)

Keuka Lake Gone With the Wind, 453 West Lake Road, Branchport (607-569-3283)

Tudor Hall B&B, East Bluff Drive, Penn Yan (315-536-3012)

Wagener Estate B&B, 351 Elm Street, Penn Yan (315-536-4591)

Bicycle Shops

Geneva Bicycle Center, 493 Exchange Street, Geneva (315-789-5922)

Weaver Bicycle Shop, 1220 NY 14A, Penn Yan (315-536-3012)

—Updated by Michael Priestman

17

Watkins Glen–Hector Wineries

- **DISTANCE:** 21 miles; easy to moderate cycling
- **TERRAIN:** Gradual ascents and descents, undulating hills, some level land
- **COUNTY MAP:** Schuyler

World-famous Watkins Glen State Park attracts thousands of visitors every year, as does the Watkins Glen International Race Track, so traffic in the little village of Watkins Glen can be heavy during the summer season. Starting at the park entrance in the center of town, this route leads you out of the business district quickly and easily, to head north along a road that is not usually heavily traveled, despite its state route designation and lake view. Along this highway you'll have a chance to tour several small farm wineries, with the option of visiting three more. Most allow you to sample their products. You'll also go by the only section of national forestland in New York State, with opportunities for wilderness camping, hiking, and picnicking.

Much of the appeal of this route lies in the ease with which it carries you to scenic heights overlooking Seneca Lake and gently tilts you back down to water level again. A walk through the labyrinthine gorge at Watkins Glen State Park, with its cascades, grottoes, and dizzying heights, provides a splendid complement to your ride. You might cap your walk with a dip in the park's Olympic-size pool—a perfect ending to a perfect day.

0.0 From the main entrance of Watkins Glen State Park, cross Franklin Street

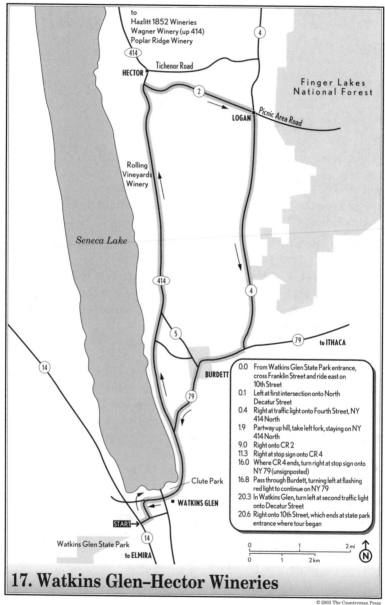

to
Hazlitt 1852 Wineries
Wagner Winery (up 414)
Poplar Ridge Winery

414

Tichenor Road

HECTOR

Finger Lakes
National Forest

2

LOGAN

Picnic Area Road

Rolling
Vineyards
Winery

Seneca Lake

414

4

414

5

79

to ITHACA

BURDETT

79

14

Clute Park

WATKINS GLEN

START

Watkins Glen State Park

14

to ELMIRA

0.0   From Watkins Glen State Park entrance,
      cross Franklin Street and ride east on
      10th Street
0.1   Left at first intersection onto North
      Decatur Street
0.4   Right at traffic light onto Fourth Street, NY
      414 North
1.9   Partway up hill, take left fork, staying on NY
      414 North
9.0   Right onto CR 2
11.3 Right at stop sign onto CR 4
16.0 Where CR 4 ends, turn right at stop sign onto
      NY 79 (unsignposted)
16.8 Pass through Burdett, turning left at flashing
      red light to continue on NY 79
20.3 In Watkins Glen, turn left at second traffic light
      onto Decatur Street
20.6 Right onto 10th Street, which ends at state park
      entrance where tour began

0   1   2 mi

0   1   2 km

N

17. Watkins Glen–Hector Wineries

and ride east on 10th Street, the street between the Tourist Information Center and the county offices.

In addition to its famous state park, Watkins Glen is known for its International Grand Prix Race Track, home to NASCAR and SCCA racing events.

There are a few restaurants and food stores in Watkins Glen. Apart from these, there are no other sources of food along this route.

0.1 Turn left at the first intersection onto North Decatur Street.
You may notice that the numbered streets in the village are indicated by small race cars with numbers on the sides.

0.4 At the traffic light, turn right onto Fourth Street, NY 414 North.
Soon you'll cross the Seneca Lake inlet, which was enlarged in 1830 as a spur of the Chemung Canal. The canal connected Seneca Lake with cities to the south. This spur extends just 3 miles to Montour Falls and is the only portion of the Chemung still maintained.

You'll also pass the Watkins Salt Company on the left, now a subsidiary of Cargill. This plant, and that of the International Salt Company 2 miles up the west side of the lake, has been pumping brine for nearly one hundred years from the vast salt deposits underlying the area. International's plant, which you'll see across the lake, looks somewhat like a power plant because heat is used to evaporate water from the brine. Sites connected with the salt industry are passed on Captain Bill's narrated Seneca Lake Cruise, which leaves from the foot of Franklin Street. It operates daily May 15 through October 15 and charges $8.50 for adults and $4 for children under 12. For a schedule, call 607-535-4541.

1.9 Partway up the hill, take the left fork, staying on NY 414 North.
The climb up from Watkins Glen is gradual and affords time to inspect the exposed shale beds, a common formation in the southern Finger Lakes. Most waterfalls in the area are maintained by erosion-resistant sandstone overlying beds of weak shale.

In about 1.8 miles you'll pass Hector Falls, known earlier as Factory Falls because of the mills, foundry, and potash works clustered here. Hector Falls illustrates a common feature of the Finger Lakes region, the hanging valley. Waterfalls resulted when glaciers downcut deeply in north–south streambeds (Seneca Lake, for example, reaches a depth of 632 feet), leaving east–west tributaries well above the new valley floors. Next to these falls is the Chalet Leon Motel, a health resort and tearoom.

Four miles farther is the Rolling Vineyards Winery, opened in 1981. This is one

*of the small wineries that have recently been springing up at the rate of a few a
year in response to a 1975 state law known as the Farm Wineries Act. Spending
only $125 for a farm winery license and $25 more for wholesale and retail licenses,
any grape owner can produce and sell up to 50,000 gallons of wine per year. The
intent of the bill—to give growers an alternative to selling their grapes at low prices
to the few big wineries—seems to be succeeding. The public also benefits by getting a greater variety and higher quality of wines.*

*Rolling Vineyards grows 18 varieties of grapes on native, hybrid, and European
vines. The winery is open for short tours and tastings Monday through Saturday 10
AM–5 PM, and Sunday noon–5 PM, May through October. Newer wineries just
beyond include Atwater Estates (about 7.7 miles) and Chateau Lafayette Reneau
(about 8 miles). A little more than a mile beyond the winery, a sign indicates the
road to lakeside Smith Park, where picnic tables are provided in secluded woodland groves and there are opportunities for camping and swimming.*

9.0 Turn right onto CR 2.
*A half mile farther north on 414 is the village of Hector. Hector was part of the
Military Tract, that portion of western New York set aside for Revolutionary War
veterans. The tract was divided into 25 townships of 60,000 acres each, with each
township receiving a classical name.*

*Those interested in visiting more wineries can continue north on NY 414. Two
and a half miles past the junction with CR 2 is Hazlitt 1852 Wineries, just north of
Hazlitt is Poplar Ridge Winery at Valois, and about 3 miles beyond that is Wagner
Winery.*

11.3 Turn right at the stop sign onto CR 4.
*A sign at the corner of Picnic Area Road in the hamlet of Logan points up the hill to
the main recreation site of Finger Lakes National Forest, the only national forestland
in New York. Although settlers tried to farm the Hector hills throughout the 1800s,
poor soil caused most of the farms to be abandoned by 1900. In 1934 the federal
government began acquiring land, reforesting hundreds of acres, adding 25 ponds
for wildlife, and establishing common pasturage. Today the Hector Cooperative
Grazing Association grazes about 2,100 head of cattle from May to October.*

*The area's recreational facilities include the Blueberry Patch Campground,
with 9 sites and 25 miles of hiking trails. There is a fee for camping at Blueberry
Patch, but camping in undeveloped areas is free. A map and further information
are available from the District Ranger, U.S. Forest Service, 5218 NY 414, Hector
14841 (607-546-4470).*

The Finger Lakes region in general—and Watkins Glen in particular—abounds with scenic waterfalls.

As you ride along CR 4, to your left you'll see the formation called the Hector Backbone rising to a height of 1,880 feet. From here the route descends gradually all the way to Watkins Glen.

16.0 Where CR 4 ends, turn right at the stop sign onto NY 79 (unsignposted).

16.8 Pass through the village of Burdett, turning left at the flashing red light to continue on NY 79.

Watkins Glen's 35-acre Clute Park at the southeast tip of the lake has facilities for picnicking and swimming, plus a small food concession. Campsites are available opposite the park.

20.3 In Watkins Glen, turn left at the second traffic light onto Decatur Street.

20.6 Turn right onto 10th Street, which ends at the state park entrance where the tour began.

In 1863 newspaperman Morvalden Ells saw commercial potential in the wet and winding glen beside the village of Watkins. Constructing a tortuous path along, above, and behind the numerous waterfalls and cascades, Ells opened what he called Freer's Glen on July 4 of that Civil War year and laid the foundation for one of the best-known state parks in the world. The site was further developed by the State Parks Commission in 1924. A free guide to the 1.5-mile gorge trail is available at the park entrance, and nightly, Timespell, the much acclaimed sound and laser light show, takes place here. The park has 305 campsites and a 50-meter pool.

Neighboring Montour Falls has further examples of gorge geology, with 20 waterfalls within a mile radius of the business district. Chequaga Falls tumbles from 156 feet above the west end of Main Street. In the Louvre in Paris hangs a 1795 sketch of the cataract done by King Louis Philippe when he stayed at the Old Brick Tavern, now a museum at 108 North Catharine Street.

Wine enthusiasts may want to visit some of the wineries on the west side of Seneca Lake. In the 25 miles between Watkins Glen and the village of Dresden are four of the region's better-known farm wineries. Because they are along busy NY 14, we don't suggest that they be visited by bicycle. With a car, however, one could spend a pleasant afternoon visiting (south to north): Glenora Wine Cellars, in Glenora; Hermann J. Wiemer Vineyard, near Dundee; Four Chimneys, in Himrod; and Prejean Winery, near Dresden.

Nearby Bed-and-Breakfasts

Country Gardens, P.O. Box 67, Burdett 14818 (607-546-2272)

Reading House B&B, 4610 NY 14, Watkins Glen (607-535-9785)

Red House Country Inn, Picnic Area Road, Burdett (607-546-8566)

Victorian B&B, 216 North Madison Avenue, Watkins Glen (607-535-6582)

Bicycle Shops

Corning Bike Works, 96 East Market Street, Corning (607-962-7831)

Geneva Bicycle Center, 489 Exchange Street, Geneva (315-789-5922)

Kingsbury's Cyclery, 228 West Water Street, Elmira (607-733-3465)

Pedaler's Choice Bikes, 13th and College Avenue, Elmira Heights (607-733-4813)

—Updated by Chip Sahler

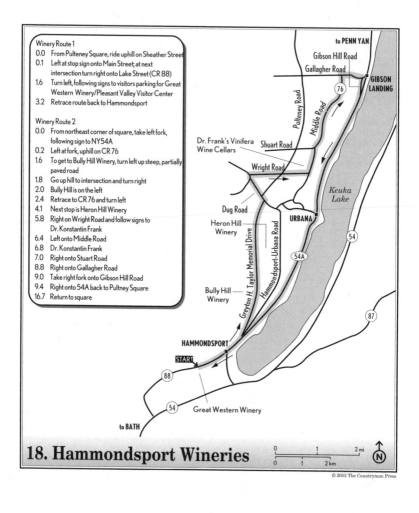

Winery Route 1
0.0 From Pulteney Square, ride uphill on Sheather Street
0.1 Left at stop sign onto Main Street; at next
     intersection turn right onto Lake Street (CR 88)
1.6 Turn left, following signs to visitors parking for Great
     Western Winery/Pleasant Valley Visitor Center
3.2 Retrace route back to Hammondsport

Winery Route 2
0.0 From northeast corner of square, take left fork,
     following sign to NY 54A
0.2 Left at fork, uphill on CR 76
1.6 To get to Bully Hill Winery, turn left up steep, partially
     paved road
1.8 Go up hill to intersection and turn right
2.0 Bully Hill is on the left
2.4 Retrace to CR 76 and turn left
4.1 Next stop is Heron Hill Winery
5.8 Right on Wright Road and follow signs to
     Dr. Konstantin Frank
6.4 Left onto Middle Road
6.8 Dr. Konstantin Frank
7.0 Right onto Stuart Road
8.8 Right onto Gallagher Road
9.0 Take right fork onto Gibson Hill Road
9.4 Right onto 54A back to Pultney Square
16.7 Return to square

to PENN YAN
Gibson Hill Road
Gallagher Road
GIBSON LANDING
Pulteney Road
Middle Road
Dr. Frank's Vinifera Wine Cellars
Shuart Road
Wright Road
Keuka Lake
Dug Road
URBANA
Heron Hill Winery
Greyton H. Taylor Memorial Drive
Hammondsport-Urbana Road
54A
Bully Hill Winery
HAMMONDSPORT
START
88
54
Great Western Winery
54
87
to BATH

18. Hammondsport Wineries

0   1   2 mi
0   1   2 km

N

© 2003 The Countryman Press

Hammondsport Wineries

- **DISTANCE:** 3–17 miles; easy cycling
- **TERRAIN:** Mostly level, with hilly optional rides
- **COUNTY MAP:** Steuben

Hammondsport is the hub of the major wine-producing region of the eastern United States. The area produces a greater variety of table wines than any other in the world. The industry was a thriving one in the second half of the 19th century, but only four companies here survived Prohibition. Today there are 5 wineries in the area bordering Keuka Lake and more than 35 in the Finger Lakes region, with new small wineries appearing each year. Informative brochures are available from the New York Wine-Grape Foundation, Elm and Liberty Streets, Penn Yan 14527.

Although five other tours in this book include winery visits, wineries are this tour's raison d'être. The tour uses Pulteney Square, the village green in Hammondsport, as base for short rides to nearby wineries, out-and-back rides, or a circular tour. Designed to visit as many wineries in as few miles as possible, the route offers short and easy excursions, allowing time for tours of each winery and for recuperation between wine-tasting sessions.

In the Dublin-based *Irish Times*, reports of arrests for cycling while intoxicated are not uncommon. Arrests for such violations are more rare in the United States; nonetheless, cycling while impaired can be hazardous—to cyclists as well as to others. Ample time should be allowed for the effects of a generous wine tasting to

Wine is aged in wooden barrels that impart flavor and aroma.

dissipate, particularly on summer days when hot air and blazing sun contrast stunningly with a cool wine cellar. And no one will take offense if you decline any, or all, of the free samples offered.

The rides start at the square in the village of Hammondsport at the south end of Keuka Lake.

0.0 From Pulteney Square ride uphill on Sheather Street, passing to the left of the First Presbyterian Church (1847).

Hammondsport earned its name as a port during the 1830s, when construction of the 7-mile Crooked Lake Canal from the northern tip of Keuka Lake to the west side of Seneca Lake linked it with the Erie Canal. Canal boats loaded with grain, lumber, and farm products were towed by steamer over the lake and thence to the canal system. By the 1850s, the construction of the Erie Railroad to the south of Hammondsport severely reduced the town's importance as a port, and by 1870 the Crooked Lake Canal was abandoned altogether.

In 1872, Hammondsport's first bonded winery, the Pleasant Valley Wine Company, built the 8-mile-long, single-track Bath and Hammondsport Railroad to link the wine village with the railroad. Known as the Champagne Trail, the little line's slogan was "Not as long as the others, but just as wide." The line still ships wine and grapes; its office is in the 1877 train depot next to the village's lakeside park. Kids swim here unofficially; sanctioned bathing is at Champlin Beach a mile from town at the junction of NY 54 and 54A.

There are several restaurants and a grocery store bordering the square, plus other restaurants around Keuka Lake.

0.1 Turn left at the stop sign onto Main Street, and at the next intersection turn right onto Lake Street (CR 88).

Wild grapes, small and often bitter, grew in the Finger Lakes for millennia before the arrival of man, but the first cultivated varieties were brought to Hammondsport in 1829 by William Bostwick, minister of St. James Episcopal Church, on a corner of Main and Lake Streets. Behind his rectory, Bostwick planted Catawba and Isabella vines from the Hudson Valley. Commercial wine production did not begin until 1860, when French winemaker C. D. Champlin founded the Pleasant Valley Wine Company and was granted U.S. Winery License No. 1. The Pleasant Valley Wine Company and its Great Western label became part of the Taylor Wine Company in 1962, and Taylor in turn was acquired by the Coca-Cola Company in 1977, which, along with Gold Seal, subsequently became part of Seagrams. In 1993, the wine brands were sold to Canandaigua Wine Company.

On another corner of Lake and Main Streets is the library and the Glenn H. Curtiss Museum. Glenn Hammond Curtiss was born among the glens of Hammondsport in 1878. As had the Wright brothers, Curtiss began his aviation career by operating a bicycle shop—his faced the square in his native village. Soon Curtiss had a bike with a motor added; by 1907 he had set a land speed record of 136.7 miles per hour in an eight-cylinder motorcycle of his own design. At the same time, Curtiss, in association with Alexander Graham Bell and others, was experimenting with flight—often at Hammondsport. A long series of Curtiss firsts and prizes followed: first preannounced and witnessed flight of 1 kilometer in America, first pilot's license, New York World prize of $10,000 for flying from Albany to New York City, operator of the first pilot-training school, first successful landing and take-off from a ship—signaling the start of naval aviation. Curtiss Company planes fought in World War I, and thousands of pilots trained in the famous Curtiss Jenny. Machines from little Hammondsport carried the name of a local boy a long way.

The museum contains many of the actual planes, hydroplanes, motorcycles, and other devices that Curtiss created, plus displays reflecting his times. These occupy several floors in what was once a school, built in 1852. Open hours are 9 AM–5 PM Monday through Saturday from May 1 to October 31, plus Sunday in July, August, and September. Admission is $4 for adults, $2.50 for students, $3.50 for senior citizens, and free for youngsters 6 and under. Mercury Aircraft, which you'll pass on the left as you ride down Lake Street, is an offshoot of the original Curtiss Company. The village and wine-country information kiosk is behind the museum.

Many of the fine homes along Lake Street were built by winery owners and winemakers during the second half of the 19th century.

1.6 Turn left, following signs to the visitors parking for the Great Western Winery and Pleasant Valley Visitor Center.
The combined visitors center is the most elaborate among local wineries, as might be expected from the largest producers. The Wine Cask theater is a must-stop. Tastings are conducted at tables in a former wine cellar. At the visitors center shop, wine, accessories, T-shirts, and more are for sale. On the spacious grounds are picnic tables and a trout stream. The visitors center is open daily 10 AM–5 PM, June through October, and 10 AM–5 PM Monday through Saturday the rest of the year.

3.2 Retracing your route out brings you back to Hammondsport.
The other major winery route takes you to Bully Hill (elevation 1,375 feet), with possibilities of side trips to another winery or two. This route is very hilly and is not for wine-weakened legs.

0.0 From the northeast corner of the square (near the Hammondsport Ambulance Corps building), take the left fork, following the sign to NY 54A.

0.2 At the fork, go left, uphill, on CR 76.

1.6 To get to Bully Hill Winery, turn left up the steep, partially paved road.

1.8 Go uphill to the intersection and turn right.

2.0 Bully Hill is on the left.
As is frequently the case in European vineyards, many Finger Lakes vineyards are on steep hillsides, often above bodies of water. The slopes provide good drainage, preventing a too-watery grape and saving the roots from rotting. Long and deep lakes give up their heat slowly, easing the danger of early frosts. Conversely, after the freezing winter, the lakes keep their surroundings cool, preventing premature budding, which could expose the blooms to a late frost. Grapes need at least 120

days between killing frosts; they can usually count on 135 in the Finger Lakes. Picking is concentrated from the second week of September through October, the most interesting time to visit the wineries—and the busiest.

Bully Hill belonged to the Walter S. Taylor family. Free Bully Hill tours, offered 9 AM–5 PM Monday through Saturday, and 11:00 AM–5 PM on Sunday, May 1 to October 31, include a tour of the vineyards, weather permitting. Also on the premises is the Greyton H. Taylor Wine Museum, a Winemaker's Gift Shop, and the Champagne Country Cafe, serving 11:30 AM–4:30 PM. Bed-and-breakfast accommodations are offered in two homes on the estate, one of which is the 1885 house of George and Walter Taylor, founders of the original Taylor Wine Company

2.4 Retrace to CR 76 and turn left.

4.1 The next stop is the Heron Hill Winery.
Heron Hill's Johannesburg Riesling won eight straight gold medals in national competition. The winery enjoys a magnificent view of Keuka Lake. Heron Hill has a gift shop and a tasting room (607-868-4241).

5.8 Turn right on Wright Road and follow the signs to the next stop, Dr. Konstantin Frank.

6.4 Turn left on Middle Road.

6.8 Dr. Konstantin Frank winery.
Dr. Konstantin Frank, originally from Ukraine, was the pioneer in growing Vitus vinifera (European) grapes in the Finger Lakes region. Vitus labrusca (native) vines (including Concord, Catawba, Niagara, Delaware, Dutchess, and more) can stand temperatures well below zero and are excellent for juice, jam, and jelly. Dr. Frank proved Vitus vinifera grapes, particularly Chardonnay and Riesling, could survive New York winters. To reach the winery, call 607-868-4884.

7.0 Turn right on Shuart Road.

8.8 Turn right on Gallagher Road.

9.0 Take the right fork onto Gibson Hill Road. Caution: This is very steep.

9.4 Turn right on NY 54A back to the Pulteney Square for a beautiful ride along the lake.

16.7 Return to the square.

Nearby Bed-and-Breakfasts

Park Inn Hotel, Village Square, Hammondsport (607-569-9387)
Rose B&B Inn, 11 William Street, Hammondsport (607-569-3402)

Bicycle Shops

Corning Bike Works, 96 East Market Street, Corning (607-962-7831)
Hillside Bicycles, 75 Bridge Street, Corning (607-936-8124)
Snyder's Wheels Unlimited, 20 West Steuben Street, Bath (607-776-6609)
Weaver Bicycle Shop, 1220 NY 14A, Penn Yan (315-536-3012)

—Updated by Tom Wood and Keith Harter

19

Steuben County Valleys

- **DISTANCE:** 28 or 38 miles; moderate cycling
- **TERRAIN:** Gentle climbs with one steep section and some level terrain
- **COUNTY MAP:** Steuben

Hidden in the southwest corner of the Finger Lakes, the valleys visited on this tour are sparsely settled. Even on a holiday weekend you can ride here through miles of sylvan quiet. About half of the tour is spent on the Whitman-Spalding Highway, a road with a wide paved shoulder and a surface so smooth that even riding uphill seems effortless. Most of the rest of the tour follows an almost traffic-free country road through the forested valley of Tenmile Creek. As there is little need to look at a map or read directions (you simply ride one road up to Prattsburg and another back), the pure pleasure of rural cycling can be enjoyed to the full.

Great things were expected of Bath, the major village here, and the starting point for this tour. Land agent extraordinaire Charles Williamson, representing the English Pulteney syndicate, laid out Bath's Pulteney Square in 1793, believing he was designing the capital of the frontier. At the head of the Cohocton River, Bath seemed sure to become a major shipping center for trade down the Susquehanna River to Baltimore. But the completion of the Erie Canal in 1825 shifted trade routes to the north and east, and population and economic growth went that way, too. Cyclists enjoying this uncrowded region will be grateful for Williamson's miscalculation.

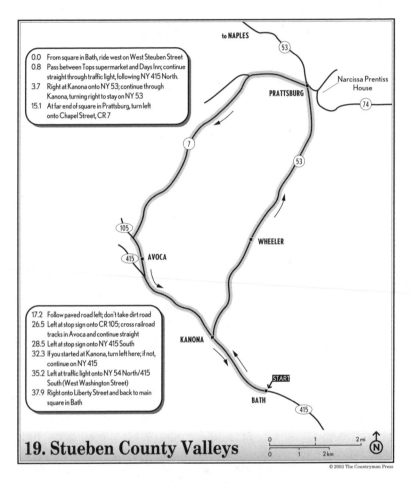

0.0 From square in Bath, ride west on West Steuben Street
0.8 Pass between Tops supermarket and Days Inn; continue
     straight through traffic light, following NY 415 North.
3.7 Right at Kanona onto NY 53; continue through
     Kanona, turning right to stay on NY 53
15.1 At far end of square in Prattsburg, turn left
     onto Chapel Street, CR 7

17.2 Follow paved road left; don't take dirt road
26.5 Left at stop sign onto CR 105; cross railroad
      tracks in Avoca and continue straight
28.5 Left at stop sign onto NY 415 South
32.3 If you started at Kanona, turn left here; if not,
      continue on NY 415
35.2 Left at traffic light onto NY 54 North/415
      South (West Washington Street)
37.9 Right onto Liberty Street and back to main
      square in Bath

19. Stueben County Valleys

© 2003 The Countryman Press

The tour begins at Pulteney Square in the Steuben County village of Bath. (The route can be shortened by some 8 miles by starting instead at Kanona, northwest of Bath.)

0.0 From the square in Bath, ride west on West Steuben Street.
Bath was honored with the name of the Pulteney family's ancestral home city in England. On its grand square Williamson established his land office and nearby built a racetrack and theater. In handbills distributed to gentlefolk from Boston to

Richmond, Williamson promised "trusty guides to meet and conduct gentlemen and their suites to the far-famed city on the upper reaches of the Susquehanna, in the land of crystal lakes and memorial parks, located in the garden home of the lately vanquished Iroquois." Clever promotion brought Bath's population to eight hundred within three years. Williamson built a mansion for himself on nearby Lake Salubria, but he was destined never to live there. Williamson was estranged from his wife, and he lost his young daughter to Genesee Fever (malaria); by 1801 his extravagance in spending a million dollars on his Finger Lakes wilderness got him recalled to England. Five years later he died of yellow fever on a West Indies–bound ship.

Bath's brief boom as a shipping center ended two decades later. Williamson's land office was pulled down in the 20th century, and little remains of his legacy save the square he designed and his little daughter's grave in the pioneer cemetery on West Steuben Street.

There are groceries and restaurants in Bath, and at the tour's halfway point, Prattsburg has a small grocery, snack shop, ATM, and a pizza/sub shop.

0.8 Pass between Tops supermarket and the Days Inn and continue straight through the traffic light, following NY 415 North.

3.7 Turn right at Kanona onto NY 53. Continue through Kanona, turning right to stay on NY 53.
Formerly Kennedyville, Kanona, or "rusty water" to the Native Americans, once constructed coastal vessels, which were floated downriver and sold in Baltimore.

Within a mile or so a sign proclaims that this road is called the Whitman-Spalding Highway, honoring two local men who became pioneer missionaries in the American West. The odd twist in the story is that Marcus Whitman was a doctor who wanted to be a minister, and Henry Spalding was a minister who wanted the woman Whitman married. Nonetheless, Whitman and his wife, Narcissa Prentiss, and Spalding and his second-choice spouse, Eliza, set out together to the Oregon Territory in 1836, the women becoming the first whites of their gender to cross the Rockies.

About 4 miles from Kanona is the hamlet of Wheeler, where Dr. Whitman worked for several years as a young physician. Here the Wheeler Bed and Breakfast, on the right, provides accommodations in an 1867 Greek Revival home.

15.1 At the far end of the square in Prattsburg, turn left onto Chapel Street, CR 7.
CR 7 provides a beautiful ride, but ride knowing that (at the time of this update)

Some veterans who had first seen the Finger Lakes region during the Revolutionary War lie buried in its cemeteries.

SALLY WALTERS

*the road surface is average, there is no shoulder, and the road edge is very rough
and broken.*

*Narcissa Prentiss and Henry Spalding attended the Franklin Academy in
Prattsburg. The house in which she was born and spent her early years is open to the
public Saturday, Sunday, and holidays, June 1 to September 30, 1–5 PM. To see it, turn
right (east) at the green onto Mechanic Street. Travel 0.5 mile as the road bears right
toward Pulteney. Turn left at CR 75; the house is the first one on the right.*

*The Prentiss house was probably the first frame dwelling in the area. There
Narcissa seems to have absorbed a sense of religious purpose from parents said
never to laugh for fear of appearing frivolous. Her missionary zeal was formed
independent of Dr. Whitman. She asked the Presbyterian Missionary Board if
unmarried females were wanted; at about that time Whitman was planning a long
westward expedition and settlement. Each could well use a spouse-companion.
Their honeymoon trip included the Spaldings and assorted fur company traders; it
lasted 2,250 miles and involved hauling the first wagon over what was to be called
the Oregon Trail.*

*In 1847, near Walla Walla, Washington, Dr. Whitman, his wife, and 12 other
whites were killed by Cayuse Indians—directly, because they were blamed for a
deadly measles epidemic; perhaps indirectly, because of rage that the Native
American way of life was being erased from the country. Henry Spalding had
spent the previous night at the Whitmans' house and escaped by only hours. He
lived to be an old man and died in Idaho.*

*When you leave Prattsburg, the rather tough uphill lasts for 1.5 miles, climbing
to more than 2,100 feet. But once the climb is over, you have a wonderful, miles-
long downhill.*

17.2 Follow the paved road to the left; don't take the dirt road.
*The valley of Tenmile Creek has only a few small farmsteads. The largely hardwood
forest is bright orange-red in autumn.*

26.5 Turn left at the stop sign onto CR 105. In the village of Avoca, cross the
railroad tracks and continue straight through town.
*Once called Podunk, Avoca's name was changed to grant the dying wish of a
resident.*

28.5 At the stop sign, turn left onto NY 415 South.

32.3 If you started at Kanona, turn left here into the village. If not, continue
on NY 415 toward Bath.

35.2 At the traffic light, turn left onto NY 54 North/415 South (West Washington Street).

37.9 Turn right onto Liberty Street. This brings you back to the main square in Bath in a few blocks.
Bath's modern Days Inn has a swimming pool and a restaurant.

To learn more about Bath, you can visit the village museum, Elm Cottage (607-776-9930), at 28 Cameron Street, south of the river. In July and August it is open Monday through Friday, 10 AM–noon and 1–3 PM. On the way you'll pass the town library, established in a fine 1829 building that was once the home of railroad magnate John Magee.

Nearby Accommodations

Days Inn of Bath, 330 West Morris Street, Bath (607-776-7644)
Wheeler Bed and Breakfast, RD 2, Box 455, Bath (607-776-6576)

Bicycle Shops

Corning Bike Works, 96 East Market Street, Corning (607-962-7831)
Hillside Bicycles, 75 Bridge Street, Corning (607-936-8124)
Snyder's Wheels Unlimited, 20 West Steuben Street, Bath (607-776-6609)

—Updated by Chris Dombrowski

Corning–Harris Hill

- **DISTANCE:** 32 miles; easy cycling
- **TERRAIN:** Flat terrain, with one big hill
- **COUNTY MAPS:** Chemung, Steuben

All of this tour is in the wide, flat valley of the Chemung River except (there's always a catch, isn't there?) for one big hill. Harris Hill rises steeply 700 feet from the valley floor. On its breezy top you'd expect to find kids flying kites or tossing model airplanes into the wind—and in a way that's true. This hill is known as the Glider Capital of America, the traditional center for sailplane enthusiasts. A sleek, modern building houses the National Soaring Museum, where the latest display techniques and audiovisual devices explain the history and mystery of soaring. Sailplanes take off and land in front of the museum; if you go for a ride in a two-seater, it will surely be the high point of your trip. More mundane pleasures in Harris Hill Park include an excellent swimming pool.

The tour begins in the city of Corning, with its famous Corning Glass Works, home of Steuben Glass. The Museum of Glass deserves all the superlatives it has received. Simply, it shouldn't be missed. And downtown Corning is a very pleasant surprise, having benefited from one of the most innovative and successful renewal efforts of recent years. Anyone remembering Corning before the 1972 flood will be amazed.

The modern buildings at the end of Market Street are limited in height to harmonize with the old shops. The Radisson Inn is

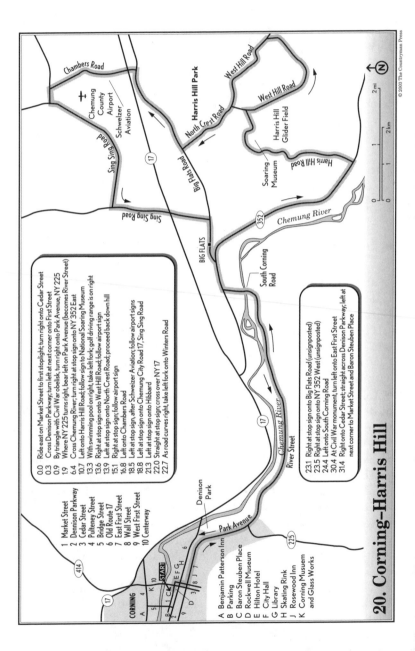

20. Corning–Harris Hill

CORNING

1 Market Street
2 Dennison Parkway
3 Cedar Street
4 Pulteney Street
5 Bridge Street
6 Old Route 17
7 East First Street
8 Wall Street
9 West First Street
10 Centerway

A Benjamin Patterson Inn
B Parking
C Baron Steuben Place
D Rockwell Museum
E Hilton Hotel
F City Hall
G Library
H Skating Rink
J Rosewood Inn
K Corning Musuem and Glass Works

Denison Park

Park Avenue

River Street

Chemung River

South Corning Road

BIG FLATS

Chemung River

Sing Sing Road

Sing Sing Road

Chambers Road

Chemung County Airport

Schweizer Aviation

Big Flats Road

North Crest Road

West Hill Road

West Hill Road

North Harris Hill Park

Harris Hill Glider Field

Soaring Museum

Harris Hill Road

Chemung River

0.0	Ride east on Market Street to first stoplight; turn right onto Cedar Street
0.3	Cross Denison Parkway; turn left at next corner onto First Street
0.9	By triangle with Civil War obelisk, turn right onto Park Avenue, NY 225
1.9	Where NY 225 turns right, bear left on Park Avenue (becomes River Street)
6.4	Cross Chemung River; turn right at stop sign onto NY 352 East
10.7	Left onto Harris Hill Road; follow sign to National Soaring Museum
13.3	With swimming pool on right, take left fork; golf driving range is on right
13.6	Right at stop sign on West Hill Road; follow airport sign
13.9	Left at stop sign onto North Crest Road; proceed back down hill
15.1	Right at stop sign; follow airport sign
16.8	Left onto Chambers Road
18.5	Left at stop sign, after Schweizer Aviation; follow airport signs
18.8	Left at stop sign onto Chemung City Road 17, Sing Sing Road
21.3	Left at stop sign onto Hibbard
22.0	Straight at stop sign; cross over NY 17
22.7	As road curves right, take left fork onto Winters Road
23.1	Right at stop sign on Big Flats Road (unsignposted)
23.5	Right at stop sign on NY 352 West (unsignposted)
24.4	Left onto South Corning Road
30.4	At Civil War monument, turn left onto East First Street
31.4	Right onto Cedar Street; straight across Denison Parkway; left at next corner to Market Street and Baron Steuben Place

N

2 mi

© 2003 The Countryman Press

A farm in the Chemung River Valley

followed by the Glass Worker's Union building and City Hall. Across the plaza is a beautiful public library; unifying the space is a covered outdoor ice rink, where you may find kids playing lacrosse in summer. A December 1976 article in *Architectural Record* has more on the design details.

The tour starts at Baron Steuben Place, at the center of Corning's Market Street restoration district.

0.0 From Baron Steuben Place, ride east on Market Street to the first stoplight and turn right on Cedar Street.

0.3 Cross Denison Parkway and turn left at the next corner, onto First Street.

0.9 By the triangle with the Civil War obelisk, turn right onto Park Avenue, NY 225.

1.9 Where NY 225 turns right, bear left on Park Avenue, which becomes River Street (also called Mossy Glen Road) outside the city limits. (Ride with caution: There is no shoulder.)

6.4 After crossing over the Chemung River, turn right at the stop sign onto NY 352 East.

10.7 Turn left onto Harris Hill Road (opposite the SPCA on your right), following a sign to the National Soaring Museum.

The uphill lasts for about a mile and a half and is the only climb on the route. At the top, where there is a spectacular view over the valley, a turn to the right leads to the Soaring Museum and the glider field. (Check the web site, www.harrishillsoaring.org, or call 607-796-2988 or hours and fees.) What most of us call gliders are more accurately called sailplanes, and purists prefer soaring to gliding to describe their sport. Old-fashioned gliders could only descend; they lost altitude slowly, but they were always on the way down. In truly birdlike style, modern sailplanes can gain altitude, soaring up on ridge or thermal lifts, like hawks.

If you go for a sailplane ride, you'll sit in the front seat, with an unobstructed view. At about 3,000 feet your tow plane dives to the left, the towrope is released, and you soar up to the right. The motor hum fades; you hear the wind. Harris Hill, forested ridges, valley farms, highways, and ponds are below. You may find a thermal, a bubble of rising warm air, and circle upward.

From the glider field, return to the main road and continue over the crest of the hill. You'll descend through lovely Harris Hill Park, with excellent picnic facilities, a snack shop, rest rooms, and a big swimming pool.

13.3 With the swimming pool to your right, take the left fork. After the turn the golf driving range is to your right.

13.6 Turn right at the stop sign onto West Hill Road, following an airport sign.

13.9 At the stop sign, turn left onto North Crest Road and proceed back down the hill.

15.1 Turn right at the stop sign, again following a sign to the airport.

W. Austin Wadsworth is one of the founders of the National Warplane Museum on the floor of the Genesee Valley, off NY 63. A few planes, including a World War II B-17 bomber, are on permanent display. But several dozen planes—landing, taking off, and flying in formation—can be seen at the remarkable September air shows. Museum hours Monday–Friday 10 AM–4 PM, Saturday 9 AM–5 PM, Sunday 11 AM–5 PM; address: Elmira-Corning Regional Airport, 17 Aviation Drive, Horseheads, NY 14845; website: www.warplane.org; phone: 607-739-8200.

16.8 Turn left onto Chambers Road.

In less than a mile after crossing over the highway on Chemung CR 35 and passing a shopping center, you'll see a sign to the left to Schweizer Aviation. Schweizer, the leading maker of sailplanes, also operates a major soaring school. Check their web site, www.schweizer-aircraft.com.

18.5 Turn left at the stop sign, after Schweizer Aviation, still following signs to the airport.

18.8 Turn left at the stop sign onto Chemung CR 17, also known as Sing Sing Road.

21.3 Turn left at the stop sign, onto Hibbard.

22.0 Go straight at stop sign and cross over NY 17.

22.7 As the road curves right, take the left fork onto Winters Road, passing under a low railroad bridge.

23.1 Turn right at the stop sign onto Big Flats Road (unsignposted).

23.5 At the stop sign, turn right onto NY 352 West (unsignposted).

24.4 Turn left onto South Corning Road.

30.4 At the Civil War monument, turn left onto East First Street.
To your right at the turn is Denison Park, which has a pond, picnic tables, grills, rest rooms, and a swimming pool. The pool is on the far side of a tunnel.

31.4 Turn right onto Cedar Street. Go straight across Denison Parkway; turning left at the next corner will bring you to Market Street. Baron Steuben Place is one block on the right.
Corning has more of interest than can be packed into one day. The Museum of Glass has one of the finest collections in the world in an imaginative new (1980) building designed by Gunnar Birkerts. Exhibits illustrate 3,500 years of glassmaking. Go to the Corning Museum of Glass web site, www.cmog.org, for admission fees and hours of operation.

The Benjamin Patterson Inn, at 59 West Pulteney Street, was built in 1796 by the seemingly ubiquitous Charles Williamson. The historical society operates the inn as a museum (see www.cruzdann.com/BPI). The Rockwell Museum, at Denison Parkway and Cedar Street, has the largest collection of western art in the East. Works by Frederic Remington, Charles M. Russell, Albert Bierstadt, and others are displayed in the skillfully restored former city hall. (Visit the museum's web site, www.rockwellmuseum.org.)

For information on shopping, restaurants, and places to stay, visit the City of Corning web site, www.corningfingerlakes.com.

Nearby Accommodations

Days Inn, 23 Riverside Drive, Corning (607-936-9370)

Radisson Hotel Corning, 125 Denison Parkway East, Corning (607-962-5000)

Bicycle Shops

Corning Bike Works, 96 East Market Street, Corning (607-962-7831)

Hillside Bicycles, 75 Bridge Street, Corning (607-936-8124)

—Updated by Alan Shepardson

10 LAKE ROUTES

Ten lakes form the heart of the Finger Lakes region, and each of them offers a different challenge to the cyclist. Some are long rides or have steep hills, while others are short and easy.

The next 10 chapters list each lake from west to east and offer the best route for circling each of them. The routes and directions suggested are designed to take advantage of the best views, easiest climbs, and most enjoyable riding conditions. A popular local feat is the "10-lake challenge," where all 10 lake routes are ridden in one season.

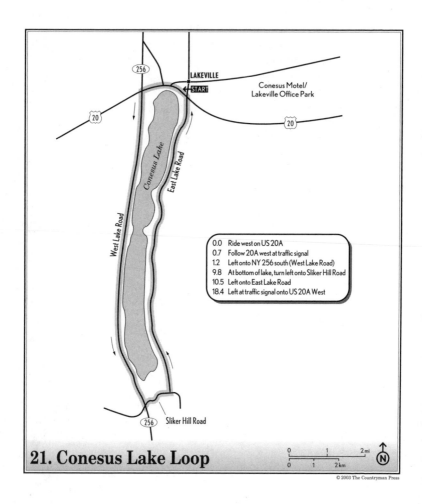

256

LAKEVILLE
START

Conesus Motel/
Lakeville Office Park

20

20

Conesus Lake

East Lake Road

West Lake Road

0.0	Ride west on US 20A
0.7	Follow 20A west at traffic signal
1.2	Left onto NY 256 south (West Lake Road)
9.8	At bottom of lake, turn left onto Sliker Hill Road
10.5	Left onto East Lake Road
18.4	Left at traffic signal onto US 20A West

256   Sliker Hill Road

21. Conesus Lake Loop

0   1   2 mi

0   1   2 km

N

Conesus Lake Loop

- **DISTANCE:** 19 miles
- **TERRAIN:** Easy
- **PARKING:** On US 20A at the top of the lake, just west of East Lake Road, you'll find the Conesus Motel–Lakeville Office Park. Plenty of parking space is available in the parking lots.
- **START:** At the entrance to the Conesus Motel

0.0 Ride west on US 20A.

0.7 Follow US 20A west at the traffic signal.

1.2 Take a left onto NY 256 south (West Lake Road).

9.8 At the bottom of the lake, turn left onto Sliker Hill Road.

10.5 Turn left onto East Lake Road.

18.4 At the traffic signal, turn left onto US 20A West. You will see your starting point about 100 yards away.

—Route by Jon Maltese

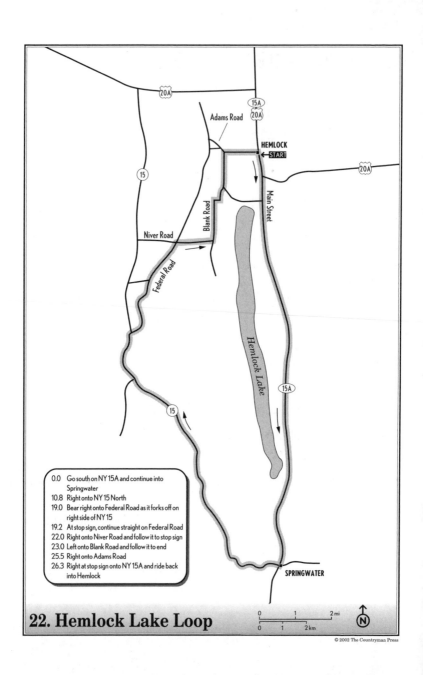

20A

15A
20A

Adams Road

15

HEMLOCK
START

Blank Road

Main Street

Niver Road

20A

Federal Road

Hemlock Lake

15A

15

0.0   Go south on NY 15A and continue into
       Springwater
10.8 Right onto NY 15 North
19.0 Bear right onto Federal Road as it forks off on
       right side of NY 15
19.2 At stop sign, continue straight on Federal Road
22.0 Right onto Niver Road and follow it to stop sign
23.0 Left onto Blank Road and follow it to end
25.5 Right onto Adams Road
26.3 Right at stop sign onto NY 15A and ride back
       into Hemlock

SPRINGWATER

22. Hemlock Lake Loop

0   1   2 mi
0   1   2 km

N

Hemlock Lake Loop

- **DISTANCE:** 27 miles
- **TERRAIN:** Moderate to difficult
- **PARKING:** Roadside parking is available along both sides of Main Street (NY 15A). If you choose to park and start downtown, it is 0.3 mile to the start of the ride east (south on NY 15A) of the village. There is also a convenience store at the intersection of NY 15A and US 20A that may provide parking accommodations.
- **START:** At the intersection of NY 15A and US 20A

This is a very pleasant and quite rural route consisting primarily of rural countryside. Hemlock Lake is closed to most uses, and development within the watershed is very limited since it is the water supply for the City of Rochester.

0.0 Go south on NY 15A and continue into Springwater.

10.8 Take a right onto NY 15 North.

19.0 Bear right onto Federal Road as it forks off on the right side of NY 15.

19.2 At the stop sign, continue straight on Federal Road.

22.0 Take a right onto Niver Road and follow it to a stop sign.

23.0 Take a left onto Blank Road and follow it to its end.

25.5 Take a right onto Adams Road.

26.3 At the stop sign, take a right onto NY 15A and ride back into Hemlock.

—Route updated by Tom Wood

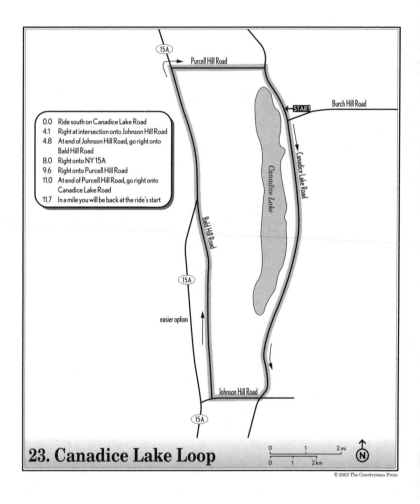

15A

Purcell Hill Road

Burch Hill Road

START

Canadice Lake Road

Canadice Lake

0.0 Ride south on Canadice Lake Road
4.1 Right at intersection onto Johnson Hill Road
4.8 At end of Johnson Hill Road, go right onto
     Bald Hill Road
8.0 Right onto NY 15A
9.6 Right onto Purcell Hill Road
11.0 At end of Purcell Hill Road, go right onto
      Canadice Lake Road
11.7 In a mile you will be back at the ride's start

Bald Hill Road

15A

easier option

Johnson Hill Road

15A

23. Canadice Lake Loop

0   1   2 mi
0   1   2 km

N

© 2003 The Countryman Press

Canadice Lake Loop

- **DISTANCE:** 13 miles
- **TERRAIN:** Moderate, with one aggressive 3-mile-long climb
- **PARKING:** On the northeast side of the lake along Canadice Lake Road, on either side of its intersection with Burch Hill Road. Canadice Lake is reached by going 3.5 miles west of the town of Honeoye on US 20A and turning left on Canadice Lake Road for 4.1 miles. Canadice Lake is a pristine, undeveloped gem in the Finger Lakes that, with Hemlock Lake, serves as the water supply for the City of Rochester.
- **START:** At the intersection of Canadice Lake and Burch Hill Roads

0.0 Ride south on Canadice Lake Road.

4.1 Take a right at the intersection onto Johnson Hill Road.

4.8 At the end of Johnson Hill Road, go right onto Bald Hill Road. This is where a 3.2-mile aggressive climb begins. (An easier option is to take a left on Bald Hill, go 50 yards to NY 15A, take a right, and meet up with Bald Hill Road at the northern end of the road.)

8.0 Take a right onto NY 15A.

9.6 Go right onto Purcell Hill Road (the steep descent after the top of the hill).

11.0 At the end of Purcell Hill Road, take a right onto Canadice Lake Road.

11.7 In a mile you will be back at the base of Burch Hill Road, where you started.

—Route by Chip Sahler

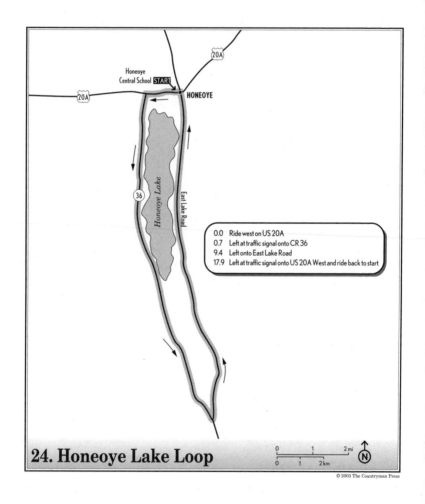

20A

Honeoye
Central School START

HONEOYE

20A

36

Honeoye Lake

East Lake Road

0.0	Ride west on US 20A
0.7	Left at traffic signal onto CR 36
9.4	Left onto East Lake Road
17.9	Left at traffic signal onto US 20A West and ride back to start

24. Honeoye Lake Loop

0   1   2 mi
0   1   2 km

N

Honeoye Lake Loop

- **DISTANCE**: 18 miles
- **TERRAIN**: Gentle rolling countryside
- **PARKING**: On US 20A, just west of East Lake Road, at the Honeoye Central School
- **START**: At Honeoye Central School

0.0 Ride west on US 20A.

0.7 Turn left at the traffic signal onto CR 36.

9.4 Go left onto East Lake Road.
The next 5 miles are winding, gently rolling terrain through forests before the summer cottages appear and the road levels and straightens.

17.9 At the traffic signal, turn left onto US 20A west and ride back to the start.

—Route by Jon Rubins

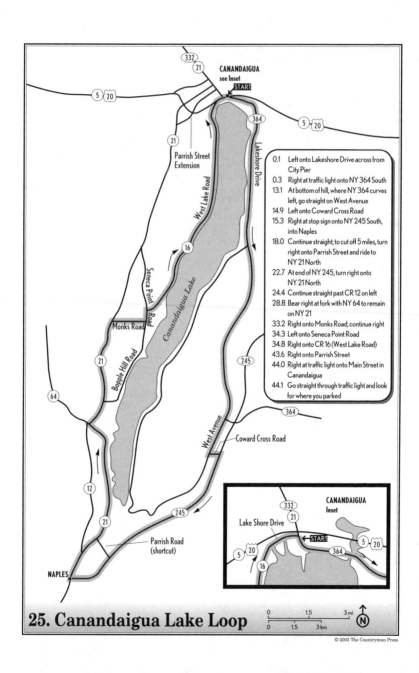

CANANDAIGUA
see Inset
START

0.1 Left onto Lakeshore Drive across from City Pier
0.3 Right at traffic light onto NY 364 South
13.1 At bottom of hill, where NY 364 curves left, go straight on West Avenue
14.9 Left onto Coward Cross Road
15.3 Right at stop sign onto NY 245 South, into Naples
18.0 Continue straight; to cut off 5 miles, turn right onto Parrish Street and ride to NY 21 North
22.7 At end of NY 245, turn right onto NY 21 North
24.4 Continue straight past CR 12 on left
28.8 Bear right at fork with NY 64 to remain on NY 21
33.2 Right onto Monks Road; continue right
34.3 Left onto Seneca Point Road
34.8 Right onto CR 16 (West Lake Road)
43.6 Right onto Parrish Street
44.0 Right at traffic light onto Main Street in Canandaigua
44.1 Go straight through traffic light and look for where you parked

332
21
5 20

Parrish Street Extension

21

West Lake Road

Lakeshore Drive

364

5 20

16

Seneca Point Road

Canandaigua Lake

Monks Road

Bopple Hill Road

21

64

12

21

NAPLES

245

West Avenue

Coward Cross Road

364

Parrish Road (shortcut)

CANANDAIGUA
Inset

Lake Shore Drive

332
21

START

5 20

16

5 20

364

0   1.5   3 mi
0   1.5   3 km

25. Canandaigua Lake Loop

N

© 2003 The Countryman Press

Canandaigua Lake Loop

- **DISTANCE:** 44 miles
- **TERRAIN:** Moderate, with three long climbs
- **PARKING:** At the southeast corner of NY 5 and US 20 and Main Street in Canandaigua. There is a large parking lot in front of some stores. While you are here, consider riding down to the Canandaigua city pier or taking a break at the lakeside at Kershaw Park.
- **START:** South exit of parking lot

0.1 Turn left onto Lakeshore Drive across from the city pier.

1.3 At the traffic light, turn right onto NY 364 South.

13.1 At the bottom of the hill, where NY 364 curves left, go straight on West Avenue.

14.9 Take a left onto Coward Cross Road.

15.3 At the stop sign, turn right onto NY 245 South, into Naples.

18.0 If you wish to cut off about 5 miles, turn right onto Parrish Road and ride to NY 21 North. Otherwise, continue straight.

22.7 At the end of NY 245, turn right onto NY 21 North.

24.4 Continue straight past CR 12 on your left

28.8 At the fork with NY 64, bear right to remain on NY 21.

30.2 *Option:* On your right is Bopple Hill Road, the toughest climb in the area, with an 18 to 22 percent gradient. If you feel like trying a very difficult climb, ride down Bopple Hill Road and climb back up.

Fortunately, the road is paved. Old-timers tell of wagons loaded with grapes being skidded down Bopple Hill with their wheels locked—otherwise the wagons would have overrun the horses.

With wet or questionable brakes it would be safest to walk down Bopple Hill, or to follow the alternate route suggested below. If you decide to ride down the hill, you should pull both brake levers with all your strength before starting down. If a cable is going to snap—and in time all cables do—you'll be safer if it breaks while you have both feet on the ground.

33.2 Take a right on Monks Road. In about 100 yards, continue to the right.

34.3 Take a left on Seneca Point Road.
About 1 mile to the right is the Bristol Lodge, with a magnificent view. It is good place for lunch or a light dinner.

34.8 Take a right on CR 16 (West Lake Road).
Just past the bottom of the long hill, you will pass Ononda Park, a lovely place for a rest and to fill your water bottle.

43.6 Take a right on Parrish Road.

44.0 At the traffic light, take a right onto Main Street in Canandaigua.

44.1 Go straight through the traffic light and look for the place you parked.

—Route by Peter Bud

Keuka Lake Loop

- **DISTANCE:** 45 miles
- **TERRAIN:** Moderate hills above the east side of the lake, then mostly level along the west side
- **PARKING:** At the Penn Yan Academy parking lot, on Court Street in Penn Yan
- **START:** At Penn Yan Academy

0.0 Take a left out of the parking lot onto Court Street, going east.

0.1 At the traffic light, take a right onto Liberty Street (NY 14A).

0.6 At the traffic light, bear right onto NY 54A.

1.3 Bear left onto CR 17 (Bath Road).
Penn Yan airport is on your left going up the hill.
If you want to skip the hills and stay close to the lake, don't turn left here. Stay on NY 54 until you reach the south end of the lake, and pick up the directions at approximately 22 miles, where you will turn right on NY 54 and head into Branchport.

13.3 Yates CR 17 becomes Schuyler CR 26.

14.4 Entering the town of Wayne, jog right across NY 230 as the road now becomes Steuben CR 87.

21.8 At the bottom of a long downhill, turn left (south) onto NY 54.

22.4 Turn right onto NY 54 into Hammondsport.

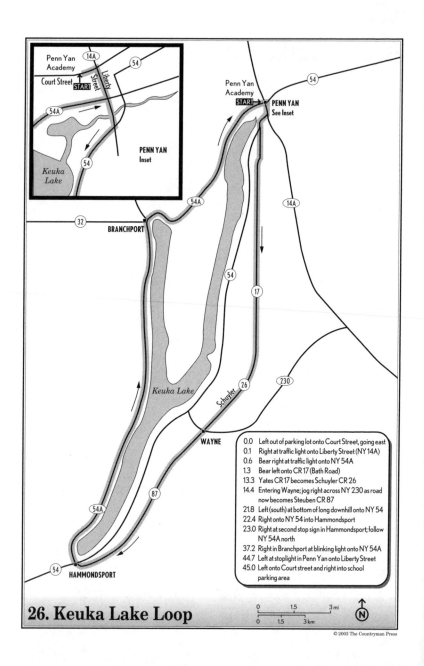

Penn Yan Academy
Court Street
START
14A
54
Liberty Street
54A
54
Keuka Lake
PENN YAN
Inset

Penn Yan Academy
START → PENN YAN
See Inset
54
14A
54
17
54A
BRANCHPORT
32
54
Keuka Lake
Schuyler
26
230
WAYNE
87
54A
54
HAMMONDSPORT

0.0   Left out of parking lot onto Court Street, going east
0.1   Right at traffic light onto Liberty Street (NY 14A)
0.6   Bear right at traffic light onto NY 54A
1.3   Bear left onto CR 17 (Bath Road)
13.3 Yates CR 17 becomes Schuyler CR 26
14.4 Entering Wayne; jog right across NY 230 as road now becomes Steuben CR 87
21.8 Left (south) at bottom of long downhill onto NY 54
22.4 Right onto NY 54 into Hammondsport
23.0 Right at second stop sign in Hammondsport; follow NY 54A north
37.2 Right in Branchport at blinking light onto NY 54A
44.7 Left at stoplight in Penn Yan onto Liberty Street
45.0 Left onto Court street and right into school parking area

0   1.5   3 mi
0   1.5   3 km

N

26. Keuka Lake Loop

© 2003 The Countryman Press

23.0 Turn right at the second stop sign in Hammondsport. Follow NY 54A north toward Branchport.

37.2 In Branchport, turn right at the blinking light onto 54A toward Penn Yan.

44.7 In Penn Yan, turn left at the stop light onto Liberty Street.

45.0 Turn left onto Court Street and turn right into the school parking area.

—Updated by Alan Shepardson

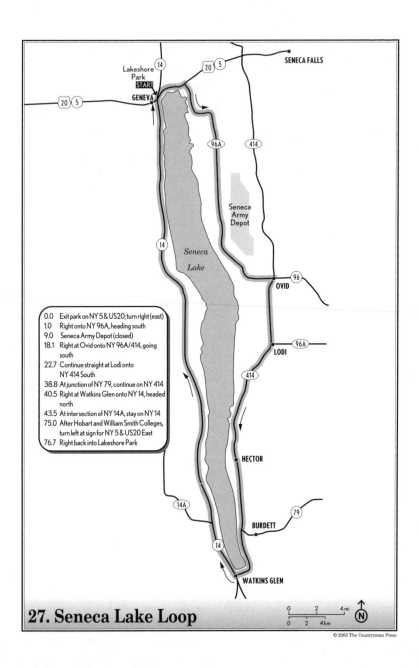

Lakeshore
Park
START
GENEVA

SENECA FALLS

20 5

14

20 5

96A

414

14

*Seneca
Lake*

Seneca
Army
Depot

OVID

96

96A

LODI

414

0.0	Exit park on NY 5 & US20; turn right (east)
1.0	Right onto NY 96A, heading south
9.0	Seneca Army Depot (closed)
18.1	Right at Ovid onto NY 96A/414, going south
22.7	Continue straight at Lodi onto NY 414 South
38.8	At junction of NY 79, continue on NY 414
40.5	Right at Watkins Glen onto NY 14, headed north
43.5	At intersection of NY 14A, stay on NY 14
75.0	After Hobart and William Smith Colleges, turn left at sign for NY 5 & US20 East
76.7	Right back into Lakeshore Park

HECTOR

14A

79

BURDETT

14

WATKINS GLEN

27. Seneca Lake Loop

0   2   4 mi
0   2   4 km

N

© 2003 The Countryman Press

Seneca Lake Loop

- **DISTANCE:** 77 miles
- **TERRAIN:** Moderate, with one long climb leaving Watkins Glen
- **PARKING:** Lakeshore Park in Geneva, at the north end at the lake on NY 5 and US 20
- **START:** At Lakeshore Park

0.0 Exit the park on NY 5 and US 20 and turn right, heading east.

1.0 Turn right on NY 96A, heading south toward Ovid.

9.0 Watch for albino deer on your left, inside the fence on the property of the closed Seneca Army Depot.

18.1 At Ovid, turn right on NY 96A/414, going south.

22.7 In the town of Lodi, continue straight (south) on 414.

38.8 At the junction of NY 79, continue on 414.

40.5 At Watkins Glen, turn right on NY 14, heading north.
This is your last chance for food and water until you are back in Geneva.

43.5 At intersection of 14A, stay on NY 14 North to Geneva.

75.0 After passing Hobart and William Smith Colleges, turn left at the sign for NY 5 and US 20 East. A right turn will put you back onto NY 5 and US 20, going east.

76.7 Turn right back into Lakeshore Park.

—Updated by Alan Shepardson

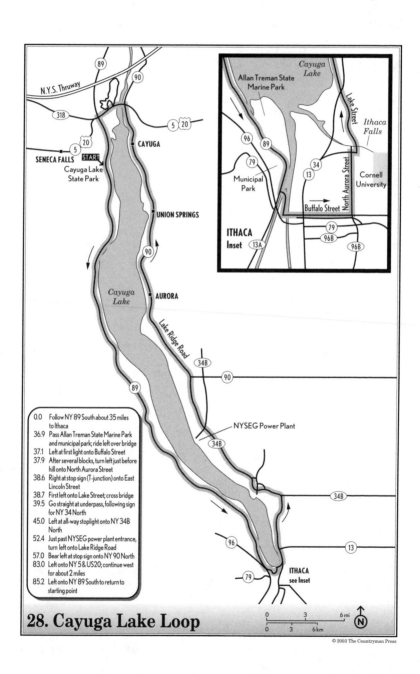

N.Y.S. Thruway

318

89

90

5 20

5 20

SENECA FALLS

START

Cayuga Lake
State Park

CAYUGA

UNION SPRINGS

90

Cayuga Lake

AURORA

Lake Ridge Road

34B

90

89

NYSEG Power Plant

34B

34B

96

13

79

ITHACA
see Inset

Ithaca Inset

Cayuga Lake

Allan Treman State Marine Park

96

89

79

Municipal Park

34

13

Ithaca Falls

Lake Street

North Aurora Street

Buffalo Street

Cornell University

ITHACA
Inset

13A

79

96B

96B

0.0 Follow NY 89 South about 35 miles to Ithaca

36.9 Pass Allan Treman State Marine Park and municipal park; ride left over bridge

37.1 Left at first light onto Buffalo Street

37.9 After several blocks, turn left just before hill onto North Aurora Street

38.6 Right at stop sign (T-junction) onto East Lincoln Street

38.7 First left onto Lake Street; cross bridge

39.5 Go straight at underpass, following sign for NY 34 North

45.0 Left at all-way stoplight onto NY 34B North

52.4 Just past NYSEG power plant entrance, turn left onto Lake Ridge Road

57.0 Bear left at stop sign onto NY 90 North

83.0 Left onto NY 5 & US20; continue west for about 2 miles

85.2 Left onto NY 89 South to return to starting point

28. Cayuga Lake Loop

0   3   6 mi

0   3   6 km

N

© 2003 The Countryman Press

Cayuga Lake Loop

- **DISTANCE:** 90 miles
- **TERRAIN:** Easy to moderate cycling with rolling terrain and several long, moderate climbs
- **PARKING:** Cayuga Lake State Park on NY 89, about 3 miles south of NY 5 and US 20
- **START:** Exit from park on NY 89

0.0 Follow NY 89 South about 35 miles to the city of Ithaca.

36.9 After passing the Allan Treman State Marine Park and the municipal park, ride left over the new bridge.

37.1 Turn left at the first light onto Buffalo Street.

37.9 After several blocks, turn left just before the hill, onto North Aurora Street.

38.6 Turn right at the stop sign (T-junction) onto East Lincoln Street.

38.7 Take the first left onto Lake Street. Soon you will cross a bridge with Ithaca Falls to your right.

39.5 At the underpass, go straight, following the sign for NY 34 North.

45.0 Turn left at the all-way stoplight onto NY 34B North.

52.4 Just past the entrance to the NYSEG power plant, turn left onto narrow Lake Ridge Road.

57.0 Bear left at the stop sign onto NY 90 North.

83.0 Turn left onto NY 5 and US 20; continue west for about 2 miles.

85.2 Turn left onto NY 89 South to return to the starting point.

—Route by John VanVechten

29

Owasco Lake Loop

- **DISTANCE:** 32 miles
- **TERRAIN:** Easy to moderate
- **PARKING:** At Emerson Park at the north end of the lake
- **START:** Emerson Park

Note: For a more detailed description of this route, see Tour 2, Owasco Lake. See also map on next page.

0.0 Ride south on NY 38, on the west side of the lake, to the south end.

15.7 Turn right at the stop sign onto North Main Street in Moravia.

16.8 Turn left into Fillmore Glen State Park. Leaving the park, turn right onto NY 38 North and retrace your route through the village.

17.9 Continue straight, north, on Main Street, which becomes Rockefeller Road after leaving the village.

28.5 Turn left at the stop sign onto NY 38A North.

32.0 Cross to the left to enter Emerson Park at the end of the ride.

—Route by Keith Harter

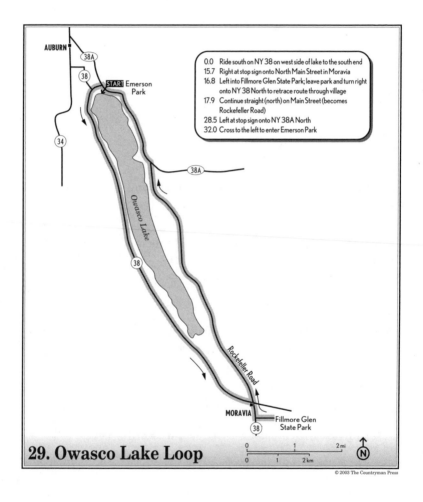

AUBURN

38A

38

START Emerson
Park

34

Owasco Lake

38

0.0 Ride south on NY 38 on west side of lake to the south end
15.7 Right at stop sign onto North Main Street in Moravia
16.8 Left into Fillmore Glen State Park; leave park and turn right
onto NY 38 North to retrace route through village
17.9 Continue straight (north) on Main Street (becomes
Rockefeller Road)
28.5 Left at stop sign onto NY 38A North
32.0 Cross to the left to enter Emerson Park

38A

Rockefeller Road

MORAVIA — Fillmore Glen
State Park
38

29. Owasco Lake Loop

0   1   2 mi
0   1   2 km

N

30

Skaneateles Lake Loop

- **DISTANCE:** 40 miles
- **TERRAIN:** Moderately difficult
- **PARKING:** In the municipal lot on Jordan Street in the town of Skaneateles. From US 20, turn onto Jordan Street. About 0.1 mile from the intersection you'll find a municipal parking lot behind Key Bank.
- **START:** At the municipal parking lot

0.0 Turn left onto Jordan Street.

0.1 At the traffic signal, go right onto US 20 West.

0.5 Turn left onto NY 41A South (Kane Avenue).

12.3 Turn left onto Glen Haven Road (in the town of New Hope).

18.0 Go right at the T-junction (Fair Haven Road will be on your left), continuing on Glen Haven Road.

20.5 Take a left at the T-junction, continuing on Glen Haven Road.

20.9 Go left at the stop sign onto NY 41 North.

38.8 Take a left onto US 20.

39.5 Take a right onto Jordan Street and return to the start.

—Route by Steve Simpson

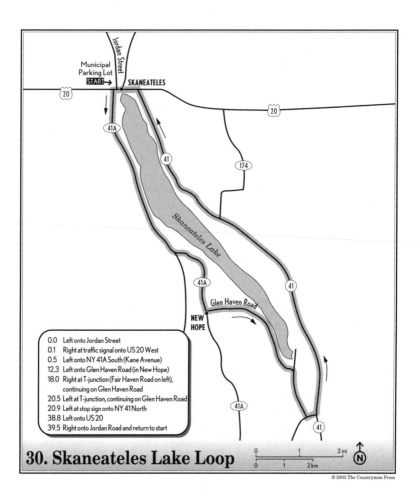

0.0	Left onto Jordan Street
0.1	Right at traffic signal onto US 20 West
0.5	Left onto NY 41A South (Kane Avenue)
12.3	Left onto Glen Haven Road (in New Hope)
18.0	Right at T-junction (Fair Haven Road on left), continuing on Glen Haven Road
20.5	Left at T-junction, continuing on Glen Haven Road
20.9	Left at stop sign onto NY 41 North
38.8	Left onto US 20
39.5	Right onto Jordan Road and return to start

30. Skaneateles Lake Loop

ADDITIONAL READING

Bicycling

Bicycling Magazine. *Basic Maintenance and Repair*. Rodale Press, 1990.

Butterman, Steve. *Bicycle Touring: How to Prepare for Long Rides*. Wilderness Press, 1994.

Cuthbertson, Tom. *Anybody's Bike Book*. Ten Speed Press, 1990.

Forrester, John. *Effective Cycling*. MIT Press, 1983.

Weaver, Susan. *A Woman's Guide to Cycling*. Ten Speed Press, 1991.

Finger Lakes Region

Adams, Samuel Hopkins. *The Erie Canal*. Random House, 1953.

Andrist, Ralph K. *The Erie Canal*. American Heritage, 1964.

Cayuga Trails Club. *Guide to the Trails of the Finger Lakes Region*. Cayuga Trails Club, 1996.

Doeffinger, Derek. *Waterfalls and Gorges of the Finger Lakes*. McBooks Press, 1997.

Dyson, Katharine Delavan. *The Finger Lakes Book*. 2nd ed. Berkshire House, 2004.

Figiel, Richard. *Culture in a Glass: Reflections on the Rich Heritage of Finger Lakes Wine*. Silver Thread Books, 1995.

Gurko, Miriam. *The Ladies of Seneca Falls*. Macmillan, 1974.

Jacobs, Stephen W. *Wayne County: The Aesthetic Heritage of a Rural Area*. Publishing Center for Cultural Resources, 1979.

Jensen, Leona. *Retreat to the Finger Lakes: Exploring the Finger Lakes for Rest, Relaxation, and Renewal*. Chapel Street Publishers, 1992.

Klees, Emerson. *The Erie Canal in the Finger Lakes Region*. Friends of the Finger Lakes, 1996.

Morrill, Arch. *Slim Fingers Beckon*. America Books–Stratford Press, 1951.

O'Connor, Lois. *A Finger Lakes Odyssey*. North County Books, 1975.

Owasco Valley Audubon Society. *Taking Time for Nature: A Guide to 25 Natural Areas in the Eastern Finger Lakes Area*. Owasco Valley Audubon Society, 1989.

Palmer, Richard F. *The "Old Line Mail": Stagecoach Days in Upstate New York*. North Country Books, 1977.

Shelgren, Olaf William, et al. *Cobblestone Landmarks of New York State*. Syracuse University Press, 1978.

Van Diver, Bradford B. *Roadside Geology of New York*. Mountain Press, 1985.

——. *Upstate New York* (Geology Field Guide Series). Kendal-Hunt, 1980.

Williams, Kevin. *For Spacious Skies: A Guide to the Unique Climate of Rochester, Western New York, and the Finger Lakes*. Weather-Track, Inc., 1993.

Maps

A detailed map of the entire Finger Lakes region is available from Map Works, Inc., of Rochester, New York. Map Works can be reached at 1-800-822-6277. The Finger Lakes Region map is $4.95 plus shipping and handling. For more information, visit www.mapworksinc.com.

County Map Sources

Cayuga County: Highway Department, 91 York Street, Auburn 13021; county clerk: 315-253-1366

Chemung County: Highway Department, Horseheads 14843; county clerk: 607-739-3896

Livingston County: Highway Department, Mount Morris 14510; county clerk: 585-243-6700

Onondaga County: Highway Department, Syracuse 13202; county clerk: 315-435-2226

Ontario County: Department of Public Works, 2962 CR 48, Canandaigua 14424; county clerk: 585-396-4200

Rochester/Monroe County: Convention and Visitors Bureau, Rochester 14604; county clerk: 585-428-5151

Schuyler County: Highway Department, South Decatur Street, Watkins Glen 14891; county clerk: 607-535-2132

Seneca County: Highway Department, Romulus 14541; county clerk: 315-549-8454

Steuben County: Highway Department, Bath 14810; county clerk: 607-776-9631, ext. 3210

Tompkins County: Highway Department, Ithaca 14850; county clerk: 607-274-0300

Wayne County: Highway Department, Lyons 14489; county clerk: 315-946-5610

Yates County: Highway Department, P.O. Box 437, Penn Yan 14527; county clerk: 315-536-5120